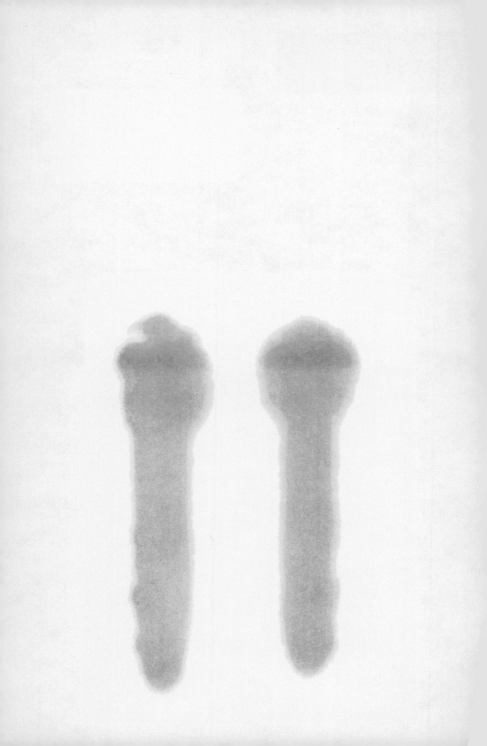

Twayne's United States Authors Series

EDITOR OF THIS VOLUME

David J. Nordloh

Indiana University

Mary Johnston

TUSAS 411

Mary Johnston

MARY JOHNSTON

By C. RONALD CELLA
Murray State University

TWAYNE PUBLISHERS
A DIVISION OF G. K. HALL & CO., BOSTON

1981

Published in 1981 by Twayne Publishers,
A Division of G. K. Hall & Co.
All Rights Reserved

Printed on permanent/durable acid-free paper and bound
in the United States of America

First Printing

Frontispiece photograph of Mary Johnston from the Mary Johnston
Papers (accession no. 3588), Manuscript Department, University of
Virginia Library.

Library of Congress Cataloging in Publication Data

Cella, Charles Ronald, 1939-
Mary Johnston.

(Twayne's United States authors series; TUSAS 411)
Bibliography: p. 156-60
Includes index.
1. Johnston, Mary, 1870-1936—Criticism and interpretation.
PS2143.C4   813'.52   80-27690
ISBN 0-8057-7340-1

Contents

About the Author

Charles Ronald Cella was born in 1939 and was reared in Carrollton, Kentucky. He received the B.A. degree from Transylvania College and the M.A. and Ph.D. degrees from the University of Kentucky. He and his wife and three children live in Murray, Kentucky, where he has been employed since 1968 at Murray State University; he currently holds the rank of Professor and is Director of Graduate Study in English.

His teaching and research interests focus upon American novels of the late nineteenth and early twentieth centuries. He has written about Washington Irving and read papers about Frank Norris and William Dean Howells. He first became interested in Mary Johnston while doing research for his dissertation about variations upon the typical young female character represented in American novels.

Preface

A generation ago Mary Johnston would have required little introduction to those who read and write about books. Even the general public might have recognized her name, for she became, somewhat reluctantly, a public figure whose travels were recorded, whose opinions were sought by the press, and whose activities in support of various causes, most notably woman's suffrage, were widely discussed. The primary basis for her fame was her prolific and, in its early stages, phenomenally popular career as a writer. Johnston published poetry, essays, short stories, a history, and twenty-three novels between 1898 and her death in 1936. Her early works sold extremely well, and most of her works were reviewed widely, sometimes receiving extravagant praise. Obituary notices, including an editorial in the *New York Times*,[1] regretted the passing of an author who had responded to and formed the literary taste of the early twentieth century.

Today she has been almost forgotten. No full-length biography ever has been published, and critical attention has dwindled to almost total neglect. Most of the scholarly treatment of her over the years has consisted of brief, somewhat patronizing references that do not represent the variety or give fair consideration to the quality of her works. In recent years, neither dedicated partisan nor objective analyst has undertaken the task of restoring to Mary Johnston some of the stature she once held.

The special challenges of Johnston's former popularity and current neglect have shaped the purpose of this book. One can no longer assume familiarity with her life or works, nor can one build upon or respond to a substantial core of previous investigations. Readers who know her work at all are likely to be acquainted with only one facet of her career or with one of the novels still cited occasionally for its historical significance.

The primary purpose of this book, therefore, is to introduce to a new generation of readers a writer who has never been examined thoroughly or understood properly. Her life cannot be surveyed adequately in a study that focuses upon the works, but the analysis in Chapter 1 of formative and continuing influences is intended to generate interest in further exploration and to summarize some of the fascinating material available for study. The remainder of the book is designed to demonstrate that Johnston's whole career and many individual works deserve renewed attention as significant reflections of the concerns of her day and as examples of the effort of a serious and thoughtful individual struggling for self-expression about topics of universal human concern. Johnston's speeches and essays are of historical interest, but her occasionally successful and often interesting works of fiction are the major topic for discussion. The high regard in which she was once held was based upon her novels, and they must be the basis upon which her future reputation will rest. Johnston is unlikely ever again to be regarded as a great novelist, for her work is uneven in quality. But it is also better than her present neglect would imply, and an analysis of the nature of and causes for both success and failure in her fiction should help restore recognition for what she did accomplish.

The plan has been dictated by the purposes. Following the chapter on major biographical influences upon the works, the next six chapters describe works which comprise major stages of her career. The order basically is chronological, even though it falls into what appears to be a topical scheme. In classifying Johnston's works by subject matter one runs the risk of dividing them by geography, and some works defy any convenient system of classification. Moreover, a chronological discussion better demonstrates the evolution of her career and explains why it prospered and declined.

Within individual chapters, the arrangement begins with introductory remarks about the stage of her career under consideration and some minor works not fully analyzed. The major portion of each chapter is given to analysis of individual novels and collections or groups of short stories. Each analysis opens with a summary of the work, including a more extensive plot summary than perhaps would be necessary if Johnston's works were better known or more readily available. Critical analyses focus upon basic elements and upon special features relevant to the context of Johnston's career; the length of discussion usually is determined by the quality or special significance of the work. Some comments by scholars and contemporary reviewers are incorporated to show both the nature and the extent of Johnston's recognition.

A final chapter traces the general response of scholarship to Johnston and provides a summary evaluation of her significance.

C. RONALD CELLA

Murray State University

Acknowledgments

My debt of gratitude extends to many persons who have provided assistance in the preparation of this book. I especially would like to thank Mary Johnston's great-nephews, John W. Johnston and Thomson Q. Johnston, who have granted permission to quote from published works and from unpublished diaries, letters, and manuscripts. Edmund Berkeley, Jr., allowed me to survey and quote from the Mary Johnston Papers (accession no. 3588), Manuscripts Department, University of Virginia Library. Misses Emma Martin and Emilie Brugh, Mary Johnston's cousins, confirmed and made vivid many biographical facts.

The Committee on Institutional Studies and Research and the Murray State University Foundation provided grants that aided materially in research and preparation of the manuscript; particularly helpful were Billy Joe Puckett and Professors Lynn Bridwell and Dan Harrison. Mrs. Betty Hornsby of the Murray State Library helped secure material of difficult access, and Mrs. Jamie Helton graciously and skillfully typed the manuscript. Initially Dr. Sylvia E. Bowman and now my editors at G. K. Hall and Co. have been patient and reassuring. Though certainly not responsible for the shortcomings of the book, my thesis director, Dr. Robert D. Jacobs, and my colleagues Dr. Clell Peterson and Dr. Delbert Wylder deserve thanks for their encouragement and advice.

I also would like to thank members of my family, each of whom contributed in more ways than I can mention here. My greatest debt is to my wife, Doris; for her cheerful willingness to help at every stage from finding sources through proofreading the manuscript I shall be ever grateful.

Chronology

1870   November 21: Mary Johnston born in Buchanan, Virginia.

1877   Great flood of James River affects family's circumstances and her imagination.

1886   Family moves to Birmingham, Alabama.

1887   Three months at Mrs. Roy's School, Atlanta.

1889   Assumes responsibility for younger brothers and sisters after mother, Elizabeth Dixon Alexander Johnston, dies suddenly on March 25.

1890   Accompanies father on convalescent tour of France, Italy, England, Scotland, and Ireland; spends first of six summers at Cobb's Island, Virginia.

1892   Father's business requires move to New York; illness restricts activities; begins to write short stories.

1896   Financial crisis causes return to Birmingham; has begun first novel, writing in New York's Central Park.

1898   *Prisoners of Hope.*

1900   *To Have and To Hold.*

1901   Sister Anne dies; has eye operation.

1902   Family moves to Richmond, Virginia; *Audrey.*

1904   Winters in Nassau; travels in Sicily, Italy, Switzerland, France, England, Scotland; introduced to Thomas Hardy, J. M. Barrie, other writers; *Sir Mortimer.*

1905   Father, Major John William Johnston, CSA, dies at Richmond in May; in June, so ill she is told she may not survive the year.

1906   Recuperates in Maryland; first of "psychic" experiences.

1907   *The Goddess of Reason;* attends commemorative ceremonies at Vicksburg; tours Scotland, France, England, Italy.

1908   *Lewis Rand;* begins extensive research for Civil War novels.

1909   Helps form Equal Suffrage League of Virginia, becoming honorary vice-president; travels in Italy, Switzerland, England, Egypt.

1910   Takes elocution lessons to prepare for suffrage speeches.

1911 *The Long Roll;* travels in France, Germany; attends Socialist meeting and suffrage convention.
1912 Speech before Virginia House of Delegates; *Cease Firing;* builds "Three Hills."
1913 *Hagar;* Equal Suffrage League in Buchanan named for her.
1914 *The Witch.*
1915 Withdraws from suffrage league; *The Fortunes of Garin.*
1916 Discusses Theosophy at Skyland, Virginia.
1917 *The Wanderers;* begins to take in boarders at "Three Hills."
1918 *Foes; Pioneers of the Old South.*
1919 *Michael Forth.*
1920 *Sweet Rocket;* College of William and Mary makes her honorary Phi Beta Kappa; declines election to organizing committee for League of Women Voters because "against any re-segregation of women"; has continuing "psychic" experiences.
1921 Switches to Little, Brown and Company because Houghton, Mifflin Company not enthusiastic about her work; fears she may have to sell "Three Hills."
1922 *Silver Cross; 1492.*
1923 *Croatan.*
1924 *The Slave Ship;* visits Jamaica.
1926 *The Great Valley;* entertains the Hindu mystic and Theosophist J. Krishnamurti.
1927 *The Exile.*
1928 Begins publishing short fiction in popular magazines.
1931 *Hunting Shirt;* attends Southern Writers Conference at the University of Virginia.
1932 Attends Southern Writers Conference at Charleston, South Carolina.
1933 *Miss Delicia Allen;* has heart problem.
1934 *Drury Randall.*
1936 Dies at "Three Hills"; buried in family plot at Hollywood Cemetery, Richmond.

CHAPTER 1

The Writer

M ARY Johnston's *To Have and To Hold* was the best-selling
novel of 1900,[1] and its popular success made her the object of
much public curiosity. Pictures and brief biographical sketches soon
appeared in various publications, all reinforcing the conclusion of a
New York Times interviewer that "Miss Johnston's life is that of
any high-bred aristocratic girl of the South."[2] If the characterization
attributed to Johnston little more individuality than the stereotyped
heroines of the kind of novel for which she first became famous, the
fault did not lie entirely with the interviewer; the writer had to rely
upon physical description and details about Johnston's family
history because she had " 'made it a rule not to talk for publication.' "[3] The same reticence is revealed in the information she
supplied for early biographical sketches. Though willing to supply
data about her family, Johnston was reluctant to discuss herself. If
the policy seems ingenuous at that stage of her career, it was
nevertheless sincere and consistently maintained throughout her
life. Johnston succeeded, perhaps too well, in her wish to divert
attention from her personal life, which perhaps is one reason that no
full-length biography of Johnston has been published.[4]

Not surprisingly, another result has been that the impression
created by early biographical sketches has not been challenged.
Writers familiar with Johnston's whole career have been aware of
her unconventional ideas and active interest in a variety of causes
but have stressed her genteel manner and Southern heritage.
Edward Wagenknecht, the scholar who best knew Johnston and
recognized the complexity of her work, summarized but did not
resolve some apparent contradictions which make her later life a
puzzle.[5] Some of the contradictions seem almost paradoxical.
Though she attempted for many years to recapture the audience
that had received her early works enthusiastically, she insisted at
the same time upon writing to please herself. Though admittedly
shy and self-conscious about appearing before the public, she made
many speeches in support of the cause of woman's suffrage. Though

she hated war, she astonished readers with vivid, authentic descriptions of battles and military tactics. Though skeptical about conventional religious belief, she devoted much of her writing career to espousal of a quasi-religious mysticism. From the earliest interviewers through the writers of obituaries and memorials occasioned by her death in 1936, all sources agree that Mary Johnston was an admirable person; it seems obvious that she also was a very complex person whose life story deserves fuller explanation.

Fortunately, Johnston provided a valuable resource for biographical investigation. The Mary Johnston Papers at the University of Virginia's Alderman Library contain diaries, memoirs, letters, and the typescript of a projected biography compiled mainly from Johnston's own words by her sister, Elizabeth Johnston. From this information it is possible to trace an outline of Johnston's background, interests, and the circumstances and events that most affected her writing.[6]

I Some Formative Influences

Mary Johnston began in March 1908 a journal in which she recorded daily events but also included many pages headed "Memory." The latter demonstrate that she believed the environment, social and physical, and some personal circumstances of her childhood had a profound and specific effect upon her development as a person and as a writer. Recognizing that her writing reflected a love of nature and what she called a "historic imagination," she emphasized the influences of her family background and region upon a child whose health and temperament made her especially aware of and receptive to her surroundings.

A. Family and Home Life

Johnston had a keen interest in her family's history and obviously assumed that her own talents could be explained by qualities of leadership evident in both ancestral lines. A notebook she kept in the 1890s contains genealogical charts tracing the lines, and her notes mention "Le Sieur de Jeanville," who "came over with William the Conqueror," and Scottish border chieftains whose loyal service brought them "the barony and lands of Annandale in Dumfrieshire" and their descendants the titles of "Earl of Annandale" and later Marquis, titles vacated "in default of male heirs."

Both the information she provided biographers and her memoirs show pride in her great-great-grandfather Peter Johnston, a Scottish immigrant who became a prominent landowner and donor of the land for Hampden-Sydney College; her great-grandfather's brother Charles Johnston, who was captured by Indians in 1790 but escaped to write an account of his adventures; her great-grandfather William Bell, an influential Baptist minister; her grandfathers Samuel Hamilton Alexander, "a lineal descendent of one of the thirteen apprentices who closed the gates of Londonderry in 1688 [*sic*]," and John Nash Johnston, " 'great in intellect as in size' "; and his cousin, the Confederate General Joseph Eggleston Johnston. Her interest extended beyond the prominent members of her family. While she was distantly related to James Madison and Patrick Henry, she wrote proudly and most frequently about less well known pioneer ancestors whose courage and endurance had helped settle the western part of Virginia.

Johnston's interest in her family and the habit of mind it suggests are everywhere evident in her work. In the most general sense they are reflected in the search for meaning in the past which she was to pursue in the historical subjects of most of her fiction. They are most intensely realized in her best works, *Lewis Rand* and her novels about the Civil War, which grew directly from a sense of obligation to her family. Lawrence G. Nelson has characterized the pattern of Miss Johnston's writing as an amalgam of a visionary and, using her own phrase, a " 'historic imagination,' " [7] and he argues convincingly that her best works reflect a tragic sense of history. The inspiration for portraying the heroic struggle against great forces which contributes to this sense of tragedy is derived from Johnston's reaction to her family's history. More specifically, that history provided a fund of material. She used her father as a character in *Cease Firing* and portions of the book to defend the military strategy of General Johnston; those are the most obvious and provable of several instances in which characters, incidents, and situations resemble her family's history.

The influence of members of her immediate family upon her career, of course, extends far beyond their possible use as prototypes for fictional characters. Mary was the first child born to John William and Elizabeth Dixon Alexander Johnston. Her father studied law in Lexington, Virginia, but interrupted his career at age twenty-two to enlist as a second lieutenant in the infantry, CSA. He fought at First Manassas and at Vicksburg, was wounded three times, and eventually rose to the rank of major of artillery. After the war he resumed law practice at home in Buchanan, Virginia, and later served in the Virginia legislature. Active in the economic reconstruction of the South, he was president of the James River-Kanawha Canal Company and held various positions in railroad companies, eventually becoming president of the Georgia Pacific Railroad Company. Her mother, whose predominantly Scots-Irish family had settled at Moorefield, West Virginia, managed the household until she died within two years after giving birth to her sixth child in 1887. Mrs. Johnston's death profoundly affected both her husband and daughter, particularly in establishing a special relationship which developed out of shared grief. Mary tried to assume responsibility for the younger children and also to fulfill the role of companion to her father. She accompanied him on many travels required by his work, and their years together fostered feelings of loyalty, respect, and love that strongly influenced Johnston's personal and professional life. She had established close family ties that took precedence over her career; she continued to live with her brother, Walter, who required special care because of childhood illness, and with her sisters Eloise and Elizabeth through-out the rest of her life.[8] Her sense of family responsibility was one cause for her attempt to become a writer; she hoped to alleviate financial distress caused by her father's reverses during the Panic of 1895. After her own success, in keeping with both law and custom, she allowed her father to manage her financial affairs.

Johnston was thus until age thirty-five in almost every respect a dutiful daughter. Her immediate response to her father's death in 1905 was a grief that extended into a prolonged illness which prevented her from writing. Her response upon recovery was to continue and expand works especially dedicated to his memory, the values for which he stood, and the cultural heritage with which these values were identified.

B. *Virginia*

Johnston was born November 21, 1870, in Buchanan, Virginia, and both the time and place had a deep and lasting effect upon her interests and attitudes. The destructive and disruptive effects of the Civil War and its aftermath lingered on and were made vividly present throughout her formative years. Her father's home had been burned when a bridge across the James River was set afire to slow troop movements, and she recorded in her memoirs that "in Moorefield as in Buchanan we yet lived in a veritable battle cloud, an atmosphere of war stories, of continued reference to the men and to the deeds of that gigantic struggle." From many childhood influences Johnston acquired not only a knowledge of the nature and consequences of the war but also a sense of loyalty to the region and the cause for which her father and her neighbors had fought. Though she never defended slavery and came to hate all war, she never believed that her state was wrong in attempting to secede from the union; it simply had asserted the right to independence it had established as a leader in the Revolution of 1776.

Thus her loyalty grew out of pride in the history and traditions of antebellum Virginia. Yet her attitude was more complex than usually has been recognized. Very much alive to her from early years, and certainly reinforced by her own family history, was a sense of special distinction about Virginia and Virginians, a sense derived in part from the tradition of a Cavalier Aristocracy and in part from the actual record of remarkable contributions by Virginians to American social and political history. That Johnston would identify with some of the ideals of her heritage, both the myth and the reality, was inescapable. Certainly both her early and late works show that she had absorbed a substantial fund of knowledge about and appreciation for what was admirable about her native region. However, her works bear only a superficial resemblance to those of such writers as John Esten Cooke and Thomas Nelson Page, who pursued a happier past to escape the wounded pride of the present. In *Hagar* Johnston shows that an unenlightened adherence to the values of the old South was responsible for the subjugation of women. Even her most romantic works do not display a blind veneration for an aristocratic ideal. Her first novel, as Jay B. Hubbell noted some years ago, was the first fiction in which an indentured servant was treated sympathetically,[9] and many of her later novels delineate sympathetically the lives of a broad spectrum of social classes in early Virginia. Johnston's knowledge of her cultural heritage was broader and deeper, and her admiration less uncritical, than one might expect from a typical daughter of Virginia. Virginia had shaped, but not inhibited, her development.

C. *Personal Qualities*

Mary Johnston's childhood temperament, intellect, and health, though not direct influences upon her writing, combined to develop interests and habits which in turn greatly affected her career as a writer. She described herself as a "diffident and sensitive child," one who was "shy and awkward, easily wounded and then too proud to show that I was wounded," but also as a child who was independent and resourceful. Her precocious and imaginative mind allowed her to listen quietly, learn quickly, and entertain herself when alone. She spent many hours alone because she was ill throughout most of her childhood. When not suffering from the commonplace diseases or the diptheria and pneumonia not so uncommon in her day, she had a combination of disorders which made her too weak to engage in normal childhood play. Frequent headaches were probably the result of an eye problem not diagnosed until her adult years, and the whole state of her health contributed to what she called "severe nervous disorders." Her only formal education, three months at a school for girls in Atlanta, was interrupted because she was too ill to continue. Illness persisted into her adult years and exerted some influence upon her work; she was often too ill to work effectively and recognized that some works were flawed because she had carried on when not physically able. One positive effect is to be seen in the strength of determination she developed in learning to live with her illnesses; that she had a writing career at all is owed to her having learned to persevere under adverse circumstances.

In spite of having spent much of her childhood in bed, Johnston remembered it as a happy time because of the kindnesses of her family and because of two compensatory influences which substantially affected her later work; as substitutes for more vigorous childhood activities, she turned to quiet walks out-of-doors and to books.

D. *Nature*

Johnston was from her earliest years deeply impressed by nature; she learned to respond to its beauty and respect its power. Her home was surrounded by flowers, and her memoirs contain long passages cataloguing the varieties. The village of Buchanan lay beside the James River at the foot of the Blue Ridge Mountains. She was allowed to roam freely over the countryside and cultivated what became a lifelong habit of long walks in the woods and mountains, savoring both the immediate surroundings and distant prospects. The river afforded an opportunity for pleasant trips aboard packet boats but was also an introduction to the power of nature; one of the most vivid memories of her childhood was of the great flood of 1877, which swept away many homes, a bridge, and the canal built by her father's company. Her own home was filled with mud, her grandmother died, and her brother Walter never fully recovered from illnesses attributed to the flood.

Other opportunities to respond to nature were afforded by frequent family excursions. At her grandparents' home in West Virginia she learned to enjoy fishing in clear mountain streams. The family often visited the sulphur-springs resorts in the mountains, and she formed an attachment which later led her to build a home there. Visits to Cobb's Island, off the Virginia coast, were especially memorable; she used her memory of the island as the setting for her most popular work, *To Have and To Hold,* and her last work, *Drury Randall.*

A continued habit of travel throughout her life provided similar opportunities. Her diaries and memoirs record several instances in which descriptions of nature in her fiction are based upon recollection of scenes not only in Virginia but in Europe and the Caribbean Islands. In some cases she visited places for the specific purpose of using such descriptions; she traveled the road to Gettysburg in order to describe the setting for parts of *The Long Roll.*[10]

The quantity and kind of examples provide insight into the ways nature affected Johnston and her concept of fiction. She said that "throughout my life, whether it shows in my books or not, has run a profound passion for nature, mystical, pantheistic"; the feelings were so strong that they could not escape the notice of any reader. So extensive and frequent are her descriptions that the natural settings become an important part of the subject matter of her novels. One writer has said that her "chief ability lay in her vivid descriptions of landscape,"[11] and the effectiveness of her descriptions of both the beauty of the landscape and the raw power of such forces as hurricanes demonstrates that observed nature was an important formative influence.

E. *Reading*

Johnston's temperament and intellectual qualities might have made her a dedicated reader even had illness not provided many hours to fill. The quantity and wide-ranging diversity of her childhood reading also were the result of her parents' indulgence of a precocious talent; she had been taught to read by her grandmother at age four. Johnston's memoirs record her gratitude for being allowed free access to her father's library. She characterized her tastes as "very catholic"; she explored, with enjoyment but not much comprehension, Juvenal, Pascal, Macaulay, Hume, Gibbon, and "an infinite variety of odds and ends." Not everything she read was of distinguished quality; she read "much of utter trash as well as much of the highest and noblest," admitted that "when I was a child I was under the spell of Charlotte Yonge," and liked the "dreadful, dreadful prigs out of Grace Aguilar." Her greatest love was for "the ballads of Scotland and Shakespeare," but she also fondly recalled Spenser, Keats, and Shelley; Dickens and Scott she "read and re-read."

The specific effects of her childhood reading are difficult to assess. She conjectured that her interest in Indian characters could be traced to her reading of Cooper, and it is easy to assume that the Romances of Adventure with which she began her career were influenced by his imitators and by Scott. However, she denied the influence of any specific literary models on her early work, citing instead her research in Virginia colonial history as the source of inspiration. Probably the primary importance of her eclectic childhood reading was to establish a love of books and a habit of reading.

The formation of that habit was both a sign of and a stimulant to an intellectual curiosity which is reflected in her adult reading. The kinds of works she read confirm the catholicity of her taste and reflect, in particular, the primary influences which shaped her adult years. She read works on sociology, the status of women, psychology, evolutionary science, metaphysics, and mysticism; she devoted meticulous study to histories, memoirs, letters, congressional reports, and thirty volumes of the Southern Historical Society Papers as she prepared to write her novels on the Civil War. Evidence of specific influence from literary works is, with one exception, difficult to ascertain. She read Hardy, Austen, Wells, Howells, Glasgow, Zola, and many others without apparent interest in imitating their modes of writing; her enthusiasm for Henry James led her to read *The Ambassadors*, which she called "my favorite," four times, but there is certainly nothing Jamesian about her work. The one exception is Walt Whitman. Johnston's love for Whitman is asserted throughout her memoirs and confirmed by various kinds of indirect evidence. The typescript of an unpublished short story, "The Prodigal Sun" [sic], obviously features Whitman as protagonist. Her poems "Virginiana" and "The River James" seem imitations of Whitman's poetic techniques; they are written in free verse and consist largely of catalogues of Virginia geography and history. Most importantly, the mystical idealism which pervades her later work could as easily have been drawn from Whitman as from any other source.

The obvious conclusion is that, with the one exception, the only influence of her reading upon her work lay in the information and ideas she absorbed. Her style and form of writing were her own variation upon popular modes, especially at the outset of her career.

F. *Becoming a Writer*

A retrospective view of childhood influences better explains the kind of writer Johnston became than that she became a writer at all; that decision was reached as a result of influences in her early adult years. Many of the influences which affected Johnston's writing career remained constant, but circumstances and events throughout the decade following the departure of her family for Birmingham, Alabama, in her sixteenth year brought some significant changes. Johnston thought herself very much interested in her father's business enterprise, which had necessitated the move, and in other contemporary economic, technical, and social developments. The novels *Hagar* and *Michael Forth* are set near enough to her own time to reflect her interest in the present.

It was during her four years in New York beginning in 1892 that Johnston turned to writing as a therapeutic relief from continuing illness. At first her writing seemed no more serious than the verses she had written as a child or the sketches of Scottish life and superstition for which she had been praised by a teacher during her brief period of formal education at age sixteen. However, for three years she wrote short stories, gradually becoming more serious about her efforts even though she did not succeed in pleasing any publishers. None of the stories survives because just as regularly as she received a rejection, she burned the returned manuscript. Nevertheless, despite failure, she developed the sense that she would be a writer and renewed her efforts in earnest when prodded by what she called the "economic spur." She said that in 1895 "we were living comfortably in an easy Southern fashion in New York. In a week all was changed. There was a sharp need of retrenchment and even when retrenchment was accomplished need remained." Her solution was to begin writing, during the summer of 1896 in

Central Park, a story she called "A Tale of a Colony." For almost two years she worked on the novel, completing it after the family returned to Birmingham. Accepted by Houghton Mifflin and published in 1898 as *Prisoners of Hope*, the novel better reflects Johnston's ties to Virginia than any of the circumstances of her life that immediately preceded it, but it was to alter those circumstances substantially.

II   Success and Its Consequences

Acceptance of *Prisoners of Hope* for publication was a complete surprise to Johnston's family and friends. She had not told anyone that she had submitted the manuscript and had displayed few signs of serious interest in a career as writer. Though only a modest success, *Prisoners of Hope* was well enough received by the public and reviewers to encourage the author and publisher to make a second attempt. The phenomenal success of that effort, *To Have and To Hold*, was almost overwhelming. It brought her fame and fortune, but it brought hazards as well as rewards.

The potential of *To Have and To Hold* for appealing to a developing public interest in historical romance was recognized early; Walter Hines Page published it serially in the *Atlantic Monthly* to boost circulation.[12] Sales of 60,000 copies in advance and 135,000 during the first week after publication in March 1900 fulfilled expectations and established the basis for sustained interest. It remains the work by which Johnston is best known and the only one of her novels still available from the original publisher.

The rewards for Johnston were both tangible and intangible. Royalties from *To Have and To Hold* alone made her, by the standards of her day, a wealthy woman; she earned over $70,000 from it, nearly $50,000 during the first year. Moreover, it guaranteed financial security for several years. Her publishers, confident that she had established a reputation and an audience, often gave her advances of $10,000 for forthcoming works. That their confidence was justified is demonstrated by the fact that, though not all were popular successes, Johnston earned over $200,000 from her first nine works. So long as she was willing to continue producing works which promised to match even partially the success of *To Have and To Hold*, she seemed assured of popular and financial success. She also was assured of the continuing benefits which attend celebrity. She was sought out by interviewers and began to receive a voluminous correspondence;[13] she was invited to speak and to write; she visited and was visited by other well-known persons. More importantly to her, Johnston was able to provide for her family both the experiences of world travel and the comfort and stability of a home. Returning to Virginia, the family lived, when it was not on tours of Europe, at various addresses in Richmond; then, in 1911, Johnston purchased a thirty-acre tract of land on a mountain overlooking Germantown (now Warm Springs) in the resort area of Bath County. The next year she built "Three Hills," which was to be her permanent home.

Popular success allowed Johnston to establish a comfortable manner and mode of living and writing, one which she later would be reluctant to give up. She was free to follow the writing schedule she preferred over the years; rising early, she wrote until others were awake. Much of her time was spent in reading, either alone or aloud in the circle of family and friends. During the years in Richmond she established many close friendships, most notably with her fellow novelist Ellen Glasgow; Johnston's diaries take note of several genial discussions of ideas and books, though neither she nor Glasgow was prompted to imitate the work of the other.

From the very beginning, however, Johnston found popular success a mixed blessing. She was prevented by shyness from fully enjoying the benefits of celebrity, and some personal crises—the deaths of a sister in 1901 and her father in 1905, and her own serious illness—compounded the frustrations she felt in having to cope with the many demands upon her time. While requests such as one for a sample of her handwriting were mere nuisances,[14] others were complications which grew directly from the commercial success she enjoyed. She spent much time negotiating about the rights to dramatize her novels and to publish them abroad and in cheaper editions. She had to meet publication schedules for novels being serialized and provide outlines of chapters not written so that illustrations could be prepared. Johnston wished to write books, not make them marketable commodities, and the accumulated frustrations were so great that she even contemplated abandoning her career.

However, that option was not available to her. She, as well as her publishers, had expectations of continued success, and their confidence perhaps contributed to her making some financial commitments she found difficult to fulfill. When she pointed out in speeches advocating rights for women that little in the rearing of women in her day prepared them to manage business affairs, she offered her own experience as example. Ironically, the greatest liability resulting from her financial success was the home it had purchased; the cost of maintaining Three Hills was so great that by 1914 Miss Johnston wrote anxiously to her publishers about advances, and in later years she and her sister had to take in boarders. Johnston's diaries and letters often record preoccupation with the commercial prospects for her works and at the same time a resentment that she had to be concerned.

The effect of popular success upon Johnston's works was therefore somewhat mixed and perhaps even negative. She recognized that continued prosperity depended upon continued popularity, and she was certainly not ungrateful for the audience her works had reached; however, she never regarded her early novels as serious works of fiction, whatever their merits, and she began to wish to be regarded as a serious writer, not just an entertainer. Responding to critical comments as well as her own evaluation, Johnston began to seek ways to please herself and at the same time meet tactful but insistent requests by her editors, publishers, and reviewers that she stay with the subject matter and techniques which had first made her a popular success.

Changes are first evident in *Lewis Rand* (1908) and the two Civil War novels which followed; though still concerned with the past and still sufficiently romantic to make them popular successes, they also reflect a seriousness of purpose which distinguishes them from the early works. They were based upon broad and systematic reading of both primary and secondary sources, and they were intended to be historically accurate. Closely identified in Johnston's mind with the memory of her father, they were written partly in response to a sense of loyalty. But they also reveal a larger purpose. Johnston was working her way toward a concept of fiction which was to dominate the rest of her career, the concept that it should not merely entertain but should be a vehicle for ideas. She never provided an explicit statement of her concept, but the chacterization "idealist-realist" she applied to the aspiring young heroine of *Hagar* (1913) is revealing. The label indicates Johnston wished to reconcile the conflicting sides of a literary controversy she perhaps did not fully understand. Her unsophisticated premise was that the writer should simply tell the truth, and her practice in the novels which followed was to include material which outraged dedicated partisans on either side. More important to Johnston than the manner of presentation was the opportunity to become an advocate for ideas in which she believed strongly.

During the last third of her career she was able to effect an uneasy compromise that partly restored the popularity lost during the middle years, as she became involved in two quite different causes.

III   *Involvement*

At the same time Johnston was discharging her duty to the Lost Cause by writing *The Long Roll* (1911) and *Cease Firing* (1912), she developed a serious commitment to some contemporary causes. She said in the autumn of 1909, "Once again there was change in the timbre and colour of my life"; the change led to involvement in the woman's suffrage movement, which in turn led to the espousal of other causes. With *Hagar* in 1913 and the three works which followed, Johnston made fully apparent to her audience the depth of her commitment.

The commitment developed after some initial reluctance. She wrote to the *Richmond Times-Dispatch* in November 1909 that she supported woman's suffrage but had no formal connection with the movement;[15] however, by December she had agreed to help her friends Lila Meade Valentine and Ellen Glasgow form the Equal Suffrage League of Virginia, and she became an honorary vice-president. Throughout the next few years she helped form and spoke before suffrage groups in many places in Virginia. She opened her own home for meetings, and the league in Buchanan was named in her honor. She traveled to several conventions and often made speeches. Probably the highlight of her suffrage activities was the momentous day when she and others were granted a hearing by the Virginia House of Delegates.

Her initial reluctance to join the movement probably could be traced to her shyness and to her sense that the movement was attempting to capitalize upon her reputation and social position. Sensationalized newspaper reports of suffrage activities, especially those of the notorious Viola Pankhurst in England, did indeed cast doubt, in Johnston's time, upon the respectability of those who challenged male dominance. To overcome her personal reservations Johnston took elocution lessons and developed closely reasoned arguments to demonstrate that demands for equal rights for women were neither ridiculous nor immoral.

The philosophical basis for her advocacy of woman's suffrage is revealed in an article she wrote for the *Atlantic Monthly* and in those of her speeches which survive.[16] While developing the expected arguments for justice and fairness, and focusing especially upon the economic injustices suffered by women, she also put the whole issue in a larger context by arguing that the evolutionary progress of both the social order and the human race was retarded by the subjugation of women.[17]

The argument reflects her developing interest in a variety of causes other than women's suffrage and anticipates the evolutionary mysticism which was soon to dominate her work; it was derived from her personal observations but especially from the intellectual influence of her eclectic reading. She read, for example, "a number of books on socialism" and found confirmation of her own "vague notions" in Lester Ward's *Pure Sociology*. Her interest in eugenics and the evolutionary development of the human race may be reflected in her reading of Darwin, but her inquiries always drifted toward the "metaphysical"; her progress from Bergson's *Creative Evolution* through works by William James, Nietzsche, Kant, and Eastern philosophy to works of Theosophy helps explain the diversity and pattern of her thought.

In addition to reading about socialism, she attended Socialist meetings and by 1912 was calling herself a Socialist, though she never formally joined any Socialist organization. In fact, she declined invitations from many organizations soliciting her support because she feared that identifying herself with many causes would dilute the effectiveness of her support for suffrage activities. However, she took interest in the reform of prisons, in improving the conditions of labor, in efforts to stop lynching, and in the humane society, contributing both money and moral support to such causes. Hating war, she mildly supported the peace movement during World War I, though, disliking the term, she refused to call herself a pacifist.

Her active involvement in public affairs actually had declined before the war began. She felt the suffrage movement had gathered sufficient momentum to no longer need her personal support, and she felt the need to devote more time to her work and her personal affairs, both of which again were undergoing radical changes. She also recognized that her involvement in causes had not helped her career.

The effects upon her work and its reception were mixed. *Hagar* was a very controversial book; among the over 300 clippings

Johnston saved one may find the novel extravagantly praised or condemned, depending upon the sympathies of the reviewer, as propaganda for the cause of woman's suffrage. Though *Hagar* sold well, the reasons were not those which had made Johnston's earlier works popular. She abandoned two projected sequels to *Hagar* because she feared that controversy would do more harm than good for the cause, but she did not abandon the cause. Instead, she subtly introduced arguments for just treatment of women into novels which focused upon other causes. Almost as heavily laden with message as *Hagar*, but more palatable to her audience because set in the past, *The Witch* (1914) and *The Fortunes of Garin* (1915) reflect Johnston's interest in religious and intellectual freedom and in social justice. She again used the historical context to emphasize women's rights in *The Wanderers* (1917), but the book was not as well received.

In deciding to become an advocate for ideas and causes, Johnston had run the risk that her message would intrude upon the fictional qualities of her novels. The four works devoted to the causes of her day display some confusion of purpose, but they retain more of the qualities of her earlier work than were recognized by her contemporary audience or her publisher. In 1918 she decided to change publishers and to take the even greater risk of devoting herself to what she had come to regard as the essence of the causes in which she believed.

IV   *Withdrawal*

Johnston attributed to herself "a religious nature, though a deeply unorthodox one," and she spent most of her adult years seeking a belief which would satisfy the intellectual and emotional need she felt. Certainly the need was not unusual, especially (though, of course, not exclusively) in Johnston's day. Challenges to orthodox religious belief, magnified by widespread popularization of Darwinian science, by questioning of the church from within that took focus in the Social Gospel movement, and—on a different level of popularization—by developing interest in various forms of mysticism made Johnston's quest an experience shared with many persons of her time. Her search was made especially interesting, however, by some personal experiences which helped prompt it, by the diversity of avenues which she pursued, and by the belief she finally chose: a trust in the inevitable evolution of the universe toward

peace, harmony, tolerance—in fact, the complete absence of conflict
in nature or human society. The fruits of her search had a profound
effect upon her life and her work; she withdrew from active
involvement in the public issues of her day, but intensified her
efforts to make her fiction a vehicle for ideas. Johnston found a
belief which brought her personal satisfaction but almost cost her a
career as writer.

Her reservations about orthodox religion were first apparent
when, at about age twenty-five, she withdrew her membership from
the Baptist church in which she had been reared. The church had
been an important part of her family history, and she knew her
action would greatly distress her father; her deference to family in
so many other matters demonstrates the depth of her discontent.
The reason for her action is less clear. Possibly it was a response to
intellectual currents of her day; no doubt she was aware of the
challenge to fundamentalist theology presented by modern science,
though her own reading of Darwin occurred several years later, and
her later interest in socialism may have grown from an early sense
that the church as an institution was not responding to human
needs. A more personal explanation can be deduced from the bill of
particulars she later developed against the church in *The Witch*.
The church is portrayed as subverting the principles of Christianity
through rigid enforcement of dogma; its persecution of dissenters
leads to fear, ignorance, and intolerance. Intellectual freedom and
tolerance of one's fellow man were concepts emphasized throughout
Johnston's work, and the frequency of references to the inhibiting
influence of religious dogma upon these concepts suggests personal
experience may have been responsible for her refusal to support the
church as an institution. Whatever the nature or source of her
doubts, they obviously did not include what she regarded as the
essence of Christianity. Instead, she regarded the Christian doctrine
of brotherly love as a key stage of development toward the all-
encompassing belief she came to espouse.

The belief Johnston thought subsumed Christianity, as well as the
messages of modern and social thought, is traceable to another kind
of personal experience, one which pointed her toward mysticism.
The drift of her thought is evident as early as 1907 when, in a diary
entry recording a conversation with Ellen Glasgow about the
Upanishads, Spinoza, and Kant, she indicated their common goal:
"To merge the self in the Larger Self and All—we both want that."
Johnston's search grew from some "psychic" experiences which

occurred during her extended illness following her father's death. At the time she regarded them as "hallucinations," but she attached significance to them as they increased in frequency over the years. Johnston characterized the experiences in an essay, "Added Space," written about 1923 but not published during her life;[18] they were experiences of tranquilly altered perception, of a heightened consciousness which she saw as a kind of immortality, transcending the limits of time and space. They became evidence to her that her own life was one stage of development of a reincarnated self and that the self would eventually merge with the universe. Johnston continued to have such experiences throughout her life, and her series of letters to Evelyn Thomson indicates she shared them with friends. A passage from one letter written 31 October 1920, when mysticism had come to dominate Johnston's work, could very well have been incorporated into her novel of that year, *Sweet Rocket:* "Yesterday afternoon I was out in the wood lying on the thick leaves, and the little 'I' seemed to dissolve into the One Life, One Will, One Mind."

Johnston's personal experiences led to and were reinforced by contacts she made while seeking explanations. She read books about astrology, numerology, and other occult sciences, and she made the acquaintance of persons with similar interests: she met Conan Doyle at the Psychic Bookshop in London, entertained and corresponded with Alfred R. Orage, who spent nine years in this country lecturing upon such diverse topics as socialism, Nietzsche, and the occult sciences, and entertained the noted Hindu mystic and Theosophist J. Krishnamurti at Three Hills. With one exception, it is impossible to determine the depth of Johnston's interest in popular forms of mysticism or the extent of their influence upon the development of her thought. Her refusal to join or allow her name to be associated with any such system suggests she shared with many other persons a kind of curiosity which did not become commitment. The one exception is the mystical belief called Theosophy. Derived from Eastern philosophy and popularized in late nineteenth-century America by the Russian noblewoman Madame Blavatsky, Theosophy stresses such doctrines as reincarnation and the evolutionary progress of the universe toward stasis.[19] Johnston had extended conversations with members of a colony of Theosophists while summering at Skyland, Virginia, in 1916 and 1917, and she maintained contacts over the years even though she never formally established ties. Similarity between Theosophical principles and the philosophy Johnston developed assure that it was one major influence upon her thought.

Perhaps one might isolate what is Theosophical in Johnston's thought from what she derived from pseudoscientific mysticism or her reading of Bergson and Whitman, but it is unlikely that she either had the philosophical sophistication or felt the need to discriminate among various forms of evolutionary idealism; for her, they all merged into one eclectic truth and, in fact, by definition should synthesize all systems. Her belief in the necessity of evolutionary progress reflects a cosmic optimism characteristic of both Transcendentalism and modern science. Her belief that progress takes place in stages of human development is exclusively Theosophical only to the extent that it depends upon a corollary belief in reincarnation. The goal of her belief, a universe of the future in which space and time are dissolved as all conflicts are reconciled, and her insistence upon tolerance as the key ethical standard for human behavior, are common to many philosophies.

The belief is ultimately so all-encompassing that it becomes incapable of precise definition, and therein lay one of the dangers to Johnston's career as a novelist. The philosophy became the main content of *Foes, Michael Forth,* and *Sweet Rocket* (1918, 1919, 1920), and her audience, already puzzled by her advocacy of causes of this world, was even more mystified by her attempts to portray a vague ideal not discernible in any world with which they were familiar. The philosophy Johnston was evolving had not appeared suddenly, having been introduced as early as *Lewis Rand,* but it remained sufficiently incidental to the main action and ideas to escape much notice for several years. The stress upon experiences of heightened consciousness and the theme of amelioration of all conflict which dominated *Foes,* however, was a major turning point in her career. Indeed, none of the works she wrote after it is wholly free from the influence of her philosophy.

The greater danger to her career as novelist lay not so much in the difficulty she had in presenting the belief as in the philosophy itself. Without passing judgment on the desirability of life without conflict, one must nevertheless have serious reservations about the potential interest of fiction which attempts to portray or even advocate such life. Fiction without conflict, without drama, is hard to imagine from the author of *To Have and To Hold,* but Johnston almost fully achieved it in *Sweet Rocket.* The quality of most of her work is inversely proportional to the extent to which she attempted to embody her philosophy in fictional form. Fortunately, a second change of publishers and the efforts of her literary agent, Carl Brandt, helped restore some of the audience she had all but lost with *Sweet Rocket*. Though Johnston never gave up the philosophy which had brought her personal satisfaction, she also attempted to return to the subjects and the methods of her earlier work; though she never again was an outstandingly successful writer in the marketplace, she did manage to produce some fiction which approaches in quality her earlier efforts.

V   *Last Years*

Johnston's mystical philosophy was the last major influence introduced into her career. Though its effect was enormous, it was balanced in the last years of her life by the reappearance of the interests with which her writing career had begun, especially a nostalgic interest in the Virginia she recalled from childhood. During her last years she wrote some short stories for popular magazines and three novels, but she recognized she had to accept her status as a " 'has been.' " She lived at Three Hills, accepting occasional invitations to speak, attending Southern Writer's Conferences, enjoying quiet walks, entertaining guests, and writing. She died May 9, 1936, after an extended illness,[20] and was buried near her parents on a cliff overlooking the James River in Richmond's Hollywood Cemetery.

CHAPTER 2

Romances of Adventure

THE works that comprise the first stage of Mary Johnston's writing career, the years 1898-1906, include those which brought her almost instant popular success and remain the best known. Though directed more by interest in the history of her region than by a desire to imitate popular trends, her choice of subject matter and the mode also coincided with a revival of interest in historical romances. Johnston's works competed favorably with those by popular writers such as George Barr McCutcheon, Silas Weir Mitchell, and Winston Churchill.[1]

Though they vary in quality, the four novels and one verse drama have in common some key features that define a type and delineate a phase of her career. The best-known of them, her immensely popular *To Have and To Hold*, has been cited by Ernest Leisy as the prototype for the category of historical fiction he calls the "romance of adventure," a type inferior to the "period novel" and the "historical novel proper" because "too much emphasis is placed on action for its own sake."[2] Indeed, the description is accurate enough to make Romance of Adventure an appropriate label for all the works Johnston produced during the first phase of her career. All are concerned with the past, specifically but not exclusively colonial Virginia, and all enact Johnston's concept of the proper way of treating history—to portray timeless, universal themes of love and honor as they develop within the personal conflicts of typical, almost archetypal, though often "real" historical characters. Melodramatic incidents and episodic plots are developed on a grand scale and played out against a backdrop of a historical setting. Johnston provides a sense of the time and place through carefully researched surface detail about the manners, customs, dress, and speech habits of a broad spectrum of social classes, but "history" is secondary in importance to qualities suggested by the terms "romance" and "adventure."

32

That she excelled in fulfilling the expectations of her early readers is demonstrated by both sales figures and contemporary reviews. What has not been clearly evident is that her Romances of Adventure also have merits which exceed the limitations of the type. They anticipate some of the virtues of her more clearly historical fiction, and they are better developed and better written than her later efforts to recapture a popular audience. At their best, they establish remarkable effects of tone and intellectual substance. When her interest in the type faded and other concerns led her in new directions, she left behind some works of lasting value.

I Prisoners of Hope *(1898)*

Mary Johnston's first novel is set among the Virginia plantations along Chesapeake Bay soon after the restoration of the Stuart line to the throne in England. Based upon a historical incident—the rebellion of a heterogenous mixture of outcasts and dissenters against Governor William Berkeley and the ruling Cavalier aristocracy supported by Charles II—the novel features historical and imaginary characters that represent a cross-section of Virginia social and political history. Against this backdrop is played out the pathetic story of Godfrey Landless, whose love for the haughty beauty Patricia Verney is complicated by his role as one of the conspirators.

Landless falls in love when he first sees Patricia, but the circumstances make him frightening to her; he is a transported convict whose indenture has just been purchased by her father, Colonel Richard Verney, a tobacco planter. Her father intends that she will marry Sir Charles Carew, just arrived on the same boat with Landless. Landless despises Carew for his elegant manners and rakish habits, but also for having taunted him about his reduced circumstances; he suspects that Carew knows he was convicted because of his support for the deposed Commonwealth. Landless holds his contempt in check until, discovered after overhearing Carew's proposal rejected by Patricia and subjected to the insult of having his apology refused, he strikes Carew.

The lashes he receives as punishment make him a desperate man, now willing to join the conspirators who have solicited his support in a plot to overthrow Governor Berkeley. He had refused to give his support because, though hating his servitude and having suffered many abuses, he distrusted the motives of some conspirators and was horrified by the proposed means—a slave insurrection.

Landless becomes deeply involved in plans for the rebellion but is torn by his love for Patricia. His position is further complicated when plans for the rebellion go awry; the idealistic leader, Robert Godwyn, has been killed by some ruthless thieves who hope to use the rebellion as an occasion to rob and plunder. Landless protects Patricia during a storm, and she thinks she has secured his promise not to join in the rebellion, rumors of which have now reached the planters. She accuses him of lying to her when she discovers him with the plotters, even though he protects her and obviously has sacrificed himself when Carew captures and kills some of them. Landless is tortured and imprisoned, but tells nothing; however, learning that the vicious element in the conspiracy, led by the mulatto Luiz Sebastian, now plans to enlist the aid of the aggrieved Ricahecrian Indians in scalping and ravishing the household of Verney Manor, Landless escapes, hoping to save Patricia. He warns the family and as proof of good faith agrees to accept all punishment for the conspiracy if others are released to help defend the house.

During the carnage which follows, Patricia is carried off by the Indians and Luiz. While Carew leads a party to pursue her captors, Landless is jailed to await the hangman. He is set free by the Indian Monakatocka, whom he had befriended earlier, and is warned that Carew is following a false trail. The two follow the correct trail and rescue Patricia, but fail to kill the abductors. Later recaptured in a bloody scene in which Monakatocka and a pioneer family are killed, Landless and Patricia escape and travel through the wilderness for several weeks. His loyalty at last is rewarded by a confession of love, but both expect to die because they have been overtaken once more. Carew arrives at the last minute and dispatches the remaining conspirators, but life is not now enough to bring Landless and Patricia happiness. Landless's offenses have not been forgiven despite his help in saving Patricia, and he must now choose between hanging and spending the winter in the forest. Refusing to let Patricia reveal their love, he sends her away with mutual promises to be true and meet in the next world.

Some early readers objected to this melancholy conclusion, but, given the characters and conflicts Johnston had developed, it is hard to imagine a more credible one. Apparently her audience, well aware of the conventions of such love stories, found most other facets of the plot acceptable. Modern readers are likely to find the primary plot one of the least convincing aspects of the book, since it relies heavily upon coincidence and melodrama. Such incidents as

Landless's discovery of the impending attack by means of a "large pebble"[3] thrown through his window and his subsequent dramatic entrance, bloody and bound, to warn the Verney household now seem more amusing than exciting, and none of the love scenes is at all persuasive. However, Johnston did handle many incidents of the plot with skill and restraint. Particularly effective are those in which the lines of conflict are drawn among Landless, Carew, and Patricia and the one in which Landless first learns of the conspiracy. And the highly charged emotional quality of some scenes is justified by the larger context of the novel: the scalping of infants would seem a gratuitous bit of violence contributing little except pathos to the plot, if it did not well establish the realities of the time portrayed.

The overall structure of the novel seems designed to reflect the historical background of the time and place, including the political, social, and religious conflicts of the day, as much as it is meant to portray a story of thwarted love. Even the chase sequence and the lengthy descriptions of costumes early in the novel are relevant to this larger context. If some incidents of the plot have an episodic quality, and if some scenes, such as the entertainment at the Verney home, are not directly relevant to it, the explanation is to be found in the fact that the plot is only one part of the larger design of the novel.

The time and place are well defined; it is a period of flux, of stark contrasts and ambiguous conflicts. The book opens with details of the personal appearance and dress of Patricia and Carew, but one quickly discovers that Johnston's purposes are not merely to portray the "atmosphere" of costume romance. She uses the details to help establish the paradoxes of Virginia life in 1663. Carew is struck immediately by the " 'curious life you Virginians lead. . . . The embroidered suits and ruffles, the cosmetics and perfumes of Whitehall in the midst of oyster beds and tobacco fields, savage Indians and negro slaves' " (3). Further details about the business interests, amusements, and social customs of the Cavalier aristocracy serve a similar double purpose and demonstrate that the contrast is greater than Carew suspects. The description of a dinner party given at Verney Manor for Governor Berkeley is an opportunity to display the manners, furniture, and even the diet of Colonial Virginians, but the political and religious squabbles which are the main preoccupation of the guests hint at trouble beneath the surface. One's impression is that the Cavalier aristocracy is an artificial civilization, genteel but fragile, in constant danger from the props which hold it up. Colonel Verney thinks that he has built a paradise in Virginia but is well aware of the danger from "Independents, Muggletonians, Fifth Monarchy men, dour Scotch Whigamores— dangerous fanatics all!" (19). It is the "d—d Oliverian element" (19) he fears even more than the Indians, who have been peaceable since the uprising of 1644, and the chief security is provided by a buffer of " 'indented servants, who are, for the most part, honest and amenable and know upon which side their bread is buttered' " (19).

It is a paradise, of course, only for the ruling aristocrats. Through Landless's experiences Johnston shows that the other side of the social order is a lasting torment for those without power. Frequent attempts of indentured servants to escape, sometimes deliberately provoked, usually result in a doubling of their term of service. Not slaves, but not free either, their feeble hope is their bondage.

Even the natural setting reinforces the picture of a troubled paradise. Establishing in her first book a habit she continued throughout her career, Johnston devotes much space to description of plants and the weather. It seems a lush, perhaps too "tropical"[4] paradise, but not for those who must toil in the fields. She skillfully depicts the raw force of nature in the wilderness chase and the storm at sea; it is a constant threat to man's fragile works.

But the primary conflict is among men. Development of the larger conflict proceeding from the conflict between ruling class and outcasts is one of the true successes of the book. At issue in the book are not just the conflicts between owner and indentured servant, Indian and settler, established church and dissenter, King and Commonwealth, but the more fundamental conflict between the individual man's right to personal dignity, whatever his circumstances, and the right of society to protect itself against the destruction from those motivated by greed, ambition, and viciousness.

The reader comes to sympathize with Landless's dilemma in choosing sides. Obviously the planters are insensitive to the feelings of the men they use as servants and slaves. They treat them as property, as beasts of burden. When their contemptuous laughter greets the legitimate request of the Indians for return of one of their brothers, the planters seem guilty of a pride that deserves to be punished. The lashes administered to Landless confirm his resolution, at that point, to seek revenge. However, he soon learns that many of his fellow conspirators are motivated by similar feelings of pride, intolerance, and selfishness, and he is appalled to discover they want not merely freedom but the opportunity to loot, burn, and kill. Johnston does not give in to the easy solution of allowing love to resolve the dilemma. Though Landless's love for Patricia influences his defense of the planters, it is not in the end a permanent solution for the conflict.

The burden of this social and moral issue may seem a heavy weight for a sometimes melodramatic Romance of Adventure to carry, and it is possible to disregard the issue and enjoy the book, as many early readers did, for its entertainment value alone. However, only by consideration of the complex issues raised may one account for the fact that the characters do not exactly fit the stereotyped roles one might expect. They are not exceptionally well drawn, but one reviewer's objection that Johnston's knowledge of human nature is "unfortunately slight"[5] is in error. Except for the pirate-to-be Luiz and the convicts Roach and Trail, there are no clear villains; except for Landless and Robert Godwyn, the martyred leader of the rebellion whose ideal of justice and freedom in Virginia foreshadows the enlightenment of the next century, there are no heroes. The aristocratic characters such as Governor Berkeley, Colonel Verney, and Carew are courtly and genteel but also humanized by their vices; they consume great quantities of alcohol, and Carew at the dinner party sings "a lyric of Rochester's" (34) which threatens to embarrass the company until the governor laughs. Carew's role in the love triangle makes him an antagonist but not a villain. Patricia, while in many ways the embodiment of the stereotyped heroine of romance, also is very much representative of the faults of her class. Her characterization of the Negro slaves as "poor silly things that are scarce more than animals" (6) is a surprising detail which adds a dimension of prejudice not expected in a romantic heroine. Perhaps most interesting among the aristocrats is Major Miles Carrington, the surveyor-general whose sympathies are with the rebels but who refuses to aid them unless they succeed. He would like to become governor but refuses to take risks; his status and weakness thus contrast with Landless's insecurity and strength. Most interesting among the rebels is Win-Grace Porringer, a follower of the "saintly Ludovick Muggleton." (55) Outraged by the Act of Uniformity, he is nevertheless totally intolerant of any sect but his own.

It is evident that Mary Johnston began her writing career with a clearer idea of character and motivation than one ordinarily finds in the Romance of Adventure. She also had a deeper understanding of the complexity of the historical and moral context of her subject than many of her readers were able to detect. *Prisoners of Hope* deserved the praise it received as an exciting tale "brim full of fire and movement."[6] It may have been an exaggeration to say that it "rises so far above its class as to occupy an almost unique position,"[7] but it does deserve serious attention as a novel.

II   To Have and To Hold *(1900)*

For her second novel Johnston turned back a few years to write a romance based upon events which culminated in an Indian massacre against the Jamestown settlement in 1622. Again grounding her story solidly in historical fact,[8] she developed an astonishingly popular tale which has as its main plot the love story of a gentleman adventurer and a disguised lady in waiting, supplemented by a cast of historical figures. The strong emotions of the characters and elements of intrigue in the plot partly explain the novel's popularity, but it has other appealing features as well.

The story is told by Captain Ralph Percy, one of the original settlers at Jamestown, and opens in 1621 with his purchase of a bride from the shipload of ninety maidens sent over by Edwin Sandys to bring stability to the settlement. Urged by John Rolfe, he decides to marry after a chance throw of the dice, but quickly has reason to regret it. He learns, after defending his new wife from an overzealous suitor and paying 120 pounds of tobacco, that she is actually Lady Jocelyn Leigh, fleeing from King James's plan to marry her to one of his favorites. Securing his promise to treat her as a guest, not a wife, she strains the limits of his hospitality and patience. His problems increase when her suitor, the beautiful but vicious Lord Carnal, arrives to claim her. Though buying time by insisting that he receive specific instructions from the company, Governor George Yeardley fears that Percy's refusal to surrender Jocelyn will further jeopardize the colony's precarious political position. Interrupting their duel, Yeardley insists upon an uneasy truce: it lasts through Carnal's attempts to abduct Jocelyn and to poison Percy, but, when word arrives supporting Carnal, Percy and Jocelyn flee in a storm and are shipwrecked. Accompanied also by his servant Diccon, by the actor turned preacher Jeremy Sparrow, and by Lord Carnal, who was knocked unconscious resisting their escape, Percy becomes captain of some pirates in order to survive. When they meet an English ship, Percy refuses to attack, fights the pirates, sinks their ship, and is arrested for his trouble, because the ship contains Carnal's acquaintances. Jocelyn defends Percy before the new governor, Francis Wyatt, and Carnal confesses his duplicity in exchange for a kiss. Returning to Jamestown, Carnal continues his machinations but at last suffers defeat. Cooperating with the Indians, who are on the verge of an uprising, Carnal ambushes Percy but is disfigured by a panther's claws. His beauty gone, and with it his chances for preferment, Carnal gives up and takes a slow-acting poison. Percy is rescued by Pocahontas's brother Nantauquas and warned of the uprising; he warns the settlement in time to repel the attack but fears that Jocelyn has been lost. His search is rewarded; reunited at last, and free to love because Carnal will soon be dead, the two make plans to return to England.

Such a bare outline of the story told by Percy may lead one to dismiss the book as merely a collection of extravagant and disconnected incidents. Indeed, the book is episodic, and many episodes strain one's sense of probability. The coincidental meeting with pirates and Percy's overcoming three of the most vicious to become captain were regarded by one reviewer as, at best, "audacious,"[9] and the intervention of the tame panther in Percy's fight with Lord Carnal is too fortuitous even for most romance. However, Johnston skillfully provides a deceptive air of plausibility in even the most improbable events, perhaps because she has them reported through a narrator who has the credibility of an eyewitness; the most improbable events do not register as such in the reading so much as when abstracted for summary.

Some questionable features of construction are less well concealed. Though Carnal's devious tactics provide a thread of continuity, the plot line involving the question of whether Percy will win Jocelyn's love is settled after two-thirds of the book, and the Indian uprising, beginning soon after, seems to divide it. Only when all the conflicts are viewed as part of the larger issue of the survival of the colony do they become unified. It was this issue that brought the maidens to Virginia in the first place, that lies in the background of Percy's conflict with Carnal, and that is brought to a head when the Indians attack. Certainly Johnston did not focus as much attention upon moral or political issues here as in *Prisoners of Hope*, but they serve as a frame of reference. The conflicts developed in *To Have and To Hold* actually are more elementary and elemental, and their being so is entirely appropriate for the colony's stage of development.

Johnston's treatment of nature as one of the forces threatening survival is a revealing clue to the larger concern. While it had been secondary to social forces in *Prisoners of Hope*, it becomes in *To Have and To Hold* a major force hostile to man's survival, and, as an element of conflict and as setting, competes favorably with the high-spirited adventure of the plot. Storms at sea and in the forest are used as devices to complicate the plot, but, more significantly, the whole natural setting intrudes upon the imagination of the characters, affecting their attitudes and the reader's. From the first page, when Percy reflects upon the death-watch quality of the brooding twilight calm and the portents of blood-red river and meteor, through his recollection of a boy made fearful by the strange Virginia landscape—"a sick fear of primeval nature and her tragic mask"[10]—and continuing throughout the novel in such details as "will-o'-the-wisps . . . pale, cold flames, moving aimlessly here and there like ghosts of those lost in the woods" (291), nature hovers ominously. The feelings evoked by nature thus set a framework within which the melodramatic plot is developed, and the skill with which Johnston evokes the mood is one of her successes.

She was not so successful in developing characters, though they have some interesting features. The characters are painted with bold strokes, with few subtleties, and, unlike those of *Prisoners of Hope*, in which even stereotyped characters are a humanized mixture of good and evil, the characters of *To Have and To Hold* are defined clearly as heroes or villains. Percy is certainly not guilty of false modesty; he makes clear that he is a shrewd judge of character, unparalleled as a warrior and strategist, and possessed of both cleverness and wisdom; he is fearless, bold, and chivalrous. He is, obviously, idealized beyond credibility. Although Johnston does provide him with a wry humor and reveals his virtues in action, the result is only to make him the most convincing of an unconvincing lot. Percy attempts to convey the impression that Jocelyn is of a beauty and character unsurpassed in history or literature: "Oh, she was beautiful, and of a sweetness most alluring and fatal! Had Medea worn such a look, sure Jason had quite forgot the fleece, and with those eyes Circe had needed no other charm to make men what she would" (35). For the reader, of course, his hyperbolic praise has precisely the opposite effect; she is indistinguishable from hundreds of other heroines of sentimental romance. Nor is Lord Carnal distinguished among a long tradition of Satanic villains; Percy thinks the moon "could never have shone upon a more handsome or a more wicked man" (179), but the reader is not convinced. His arrogance, his dissembling, his leering rage are all quite routine qualities. Johnston seems in fact to be striving, in such details as the "foam upon his lips" (75), to match a stereotype.

Her choice of name for her villain is further evidence of such intent, and it sheds light on the nature of the stereotype. She suggests, more explicitly, what many creators of similar villains expressed, that Carnal's truly frightening threat to Jocelyn, and vicariously to the reader, is sexual in nature. Jocelyn even fears Percy until he makes clear he will not take advantage of his prerogative as husband, and his self-characterization as "the best swordsman in Virginia" (23) would suggest an easy explanation to the Freudian critic. The sexual overtones here, however, and for that matter in the whole bride-purchasing scene, owe less to Freud than to Johnston's imitation of similar aspects of the sentimental novel as far back as Richardson.

Minor characters, with one exception, are equally stereotyped. Sparrow is in the tradition of the strong, loyal, ever-handy friend and companion of the hero, despite his having been based on a real person. Niccolo—again the name is an obvious clue—is reminiscent of the stock Machiavels of Elizabethan drama. The Indians seem borrowed from Cooper's stock of idealized types; Nantauquas, Pocahontas's brother, is "as brave and chivalrous, as courteous and truthful, as a Christian knight" (120), while the instigator of the massacre, Opechancanough, is "a strange and subtle savage" (119). None of the historical characters is much particularized. The one exception to the pattern is Percy's servant, Diccon. Though "meant to be the merest sketch," he displays a degree of complexity not evident in other characters; he is at the same time "an ingenious scoundrel" (32) and a loyal servant. Percy fails to understand Diccon's depths until Diccon attempts to retaliate for a lashing by stabbing Percy in the back and later, given his freedom, refuses to desert Percy. In some ways he anticipates later Johnston protagonists who are mixtures of decency and dark urges.

And so the characters seem very much to be the typical idealizations of the Romance of Adventure, but without the depth of analysis or complexity of romance at its best. Since in neither the preceding nor the immediately following novel did Johnston oversimplify character so much, her portraits may have been governed by special circumstances. The most generous interpretation would lay blame upon her narrator; it is part of his character to make quick judgments and see men in simple terms. However, there is no evidence that Johnston saw Percy as anything other than a reliable narrator.

The circumstances of publication may have contributed both to stereotyping of characters and dependence upon a plot full of exciting incidents. The novel was printed in ten installments in the *Atlantic Monthly* before being published in book form in March 1900. Since serial publication requires that interest be maintained over a long period, the writer may need to depend upon episodes with a self-contained excitement, upon suspense, and upon stereotyped characters to help readers recall what has preceded. Johnston was well acquainted with Dickens and others who were skillful in this respect.

The circumstances of writing were even more influential. Johnston told her publishers that the story developed out of her reading of colonial history; she wanted to base a novel upon the adventures of John Smith, but settled upon the incident of the imported maidens instead. Her primary concern was to establish the time and place, not to define character or tell a story. Her "puppets" evolved at first as types and then were particularized. She was content if they compared well with the stock characters of popular historical romance and if they contributed to the pictures of the times she wished to convey.

The book succeeded in both respects. The unsophisticated appeal of the exciting story and boldly drawn characters made it a spectacular popular success, and its evocation of colonial Virginia makes it of interest even today. In addition to sales figures, another indication of its appeal was the number of requests for auxiliary rights; an early reviewer's comment that "every page of the story suggests a play"[11] was recognized by aspiring playwrights who tested Johnston's patience,[12] and the novel was dramatized, rather unsuccessfully, in 1901.[13] Two silent film versions were produced, one in 1916 by the Jesse Lasky Company, featuring Follies star Mae Murray,[14] and a second in 1922 by Adolph Zukor.[15] The breadth of the novel's appeal is demonstrated in various curious ways; the poet Wallace Stevens recalled staying up "until half-past three" reading it,[16] and it has been translated into several languages, including Gaelic. Discussions were conducted in the public press about the locale of events described.[17] Johnston received congratulatory letters from fellow authors as well as the general public, and the sincere flattery of imitation has been provided by a flood of examples, most directly by Rafael Sabatini.[18]

The significance of a novel from which "a whole generation formed its picture of early days in Virginia"[19] is difficult to challenge, whatever its merits. The praise in contemporary reviews now may seem extravagant, especially characterizations of the author's style as having the "sparkle of the west wind" and the "witchery of the spring."[20] However, readers today may appreciate the material which most interested Johnston. Through Percy's reflections upon actual events of the Jamestown experience such as the "Starving Time" when men feared the cannibalism of their fellows as well as illness and hunger, she provides an authentic mood. Her description of the community itself, and the hopes and fears of those who settled it, is especially persuasive. She was not a slave to accuracy, having juggled dates to bring together the persons and events she wished to describe; the result may not be good history, but it lends credibility to the romantic plot. One must agree with Ernest Leisy that "there is truth of atmosphere sufficient for *To Have and To Hold* to rate as the best of the romances about colonial Virginia."[21]

III   Audrey (1902)

Audrey resembles Johnston's two earlier novels in significant ways, but it contains also a depth of character analysis which distinguishes it not only from her other early works but also from most popular romances. Again providing both the general and the specific atmosphere of a period in Virginia colonial history while tracing complications of the timeless theme of innocent love abused, she rises above the sentimental and conventional elements of her plot and characters to create a convincing picture of the destructive effects of improperly motivated kindness. It is the story of a young girl who is rescued from death in the wilderness only to be killed saving the man who rescued her; but it is also very much the story of her benefactor, whose self-deception leads him to interfere with her life in ways that bring misery to her, to others, and ultimately to himself.

The story opens with the arrival of Governor Alexander Spotswood's Knights of the Golden Horseshoe at the cabin of some English settlers in the Virginia mountains. Feigning injury when the explorers press on, the young Marmaduke Haward turns back to court the settlers' oldest daughter but finds that Indians have burned the cabin and killed all but the child Audrey. Haward takes

Audrey to Jamestown and arranges that she be cared for by Parson Darden, noted more for his drinking than his piety, and his shrewish wife. When the story reopens a few years later, in 1727, Haward has returned from England to attend his estates. Having forgotten about Audrey, he now plans to court the lovely Evelyn Byrd, daughter of his neighbor, William Byrd of Westover. Evelyn refuses Haward's proposal because she knows he does not love her, but he resolves to continue his suit. He overcomes the hatred of his Scottish indentured servant, Angus MacLean, whose forthrightness and uncomplicated love for the Quakeress Truelove Taberer are contrasted throughout with Haward's vacillation and contradictory impulses. Still hopeful of winning Evelyn, Haward rediscovers and becomes increasingly fascinated by Audrey, whom he is at first embarrassed to learn regards him as a "fairy knight."[22] Knowing she has misjudged him, but not otherwise understanding his feelings, he finds occasions to visit Audrey. Others, especially the vicious half-breed Jean Hugon, who wants Audrey for himself, interpret his interest as simple lust; rumors arise which compromise her reputation. Haward mistakenly thinks, despite the advice of Colonel Byrd and MacLean, that his denials are sufficient protection for her. He willfully forces Audrey to accompany him to the governor's ball at Williamsburg, where she is snubbed by Evelyn and others, protecting herself only by a suddenly discovered ability to act the part of a great lady even while miserable. Her misery increases when, accused in church, she at last learns what people think of her relationship with Haward. She contemplates suicide and is almost drowned as a witch but is saved by Evelyn, with whom she commiserates about Haward's confessed mistreatment. Thoroughly unhappy, she nevertheless makes a life and a reputation as a tragic actress upon the Williamsburg stage. Haward at last promises to leave her alone because she does not love him; however, she says she does, and all seems well at last. Their happiness is shortlived because she is stabbed when attempting to protect Haward from Hugon's attack.

While obviously melodramatic and episodic, and perhaps reflecting the same influences of popular romance and serialization which affected *To Have and To Hold*, *Audrey* has as its most striking feature a theatrical quality. Many incidents seem contrived as scenes for stage presentation.

Melodrama is most conspicuous in such scenes as those at the church and the ball, in which the reader recognizes Audrey as the epitome of innocence wrongfully accused. Some scenes, such as

Audrey's rescue of Haward and Colonel Byrd from ambush and Haward's swordplay with MacLean, remind one of similar melodramatic moments in the earlier novels. The final scene, in which Audrey sacrifices herself for Haward, is especially calculated to provoke strong emotion. However, the same stagelike quality is present throughout the book in many scenes that do not provoke strong emotions. Some are contrived to display in full array the customs of colonial life and some to establish Audrey's close ties to nature. The May Day festivities at which Haward sees Audrey for the first time in several years and his meeting with her in her garden fulfill these purposes, and they leave a distinct impression of having been written with a view toward dramatization. Such a prospect would not have been unreasonable to expect, since preparations were being made to dramatize *To Have and To Hold* when *Audrey* was written, and indeed *Audrey* was dramatized by Harriet Ford in 1902.[23] An actress in the road company which toured the South described Johnston as enthralled by seeing her characters brought to life,[24] and she may have been a witness to the fulfillment of her intentions while writing.

A less conjectural explanation for the theatrical quality of the novel is to be found in its subject matter. Since considerable portions of the novel are devoted to describing the theater of colonial Williamsburg, including information about which plays were popular, about styles of acting, and even about circumstances of production,[25] it would be surprising if the novel were not significantly influenced by Johnston's study of the subject.

Whatever the explanation, the scenes and method also afforded Johnston an opportunity to display much of the life of eighteenth-century Virginia. One sees early the merriment and fine talk of the party of explorers, and the May Day Celebration in Jamestown shows a society which in its amusements has closely imitated the latest English fashions. It is not so elegant as the newly arrived Haward, but it struggles not to be provincial. However, Johnston also shows that Jamestown is losing out to Williamsburg as the center of culture and refinement; MacLean and Hugon's excursion there is used to describe a scene now familiar to thousands of tourists who have visited the Williamsburg Restoration, begun some thirty years after the novel was published. The manners and customs of the community are displayed in scenes at taverns and in church, and the festivities of one week (though not all portrayed) are listed to show the diversity of amusements; included are a ball for the new governor, a public hanging of some pirates, and a performance of Addison's *Cato*. Other details, such as references to the "planter's pace," a full-speed gallop, and a list of items in Haward's store, provide a sense of Virginia social history. Parson Darden's drinking habits and MacLean's courtship of the pious Truelove show contrasting sides of the social order both different from the life of the aristocratic Byrd family.

The use of historical characters such as the Byrd family involved some risks but clearly contributed to the success of the novel. Many writers of historical romance do not integrate such characters into the action, but instead offer mere stage props introduced in improbable fashion to lend an air of authenticity to an otherwise incredible plot. (Indeed, some of the characters in *To Have and To Hold*, such as John Rolfe, are not essential to the plot.) However, in *Audrey*, Johnston skillfully ties together history, legend, and ficton in the character Evelyn Byrd. The legend of her death from a broken heart—a legend which grew because of the poem on her gravestone in Westover churchyard—is unobtrusively present in her unhappy relations with Haward, but Johnston never makes the mistake of explaining too much. If Evelyn Byrd is not fully believable as a character, the failure is the result of her idealization as a woman, not as a historical figure; Johnston handles rather well the difficult task of making her at the same time a sympathetic character and one who hurts the feelings of the heroine Audrey. Her contribution to the novel is as a character, not as a historical person.

The portrait of Audrey was an even more ambitious effort, and the result, considering the astonishing combination of qualities she is supposed to represent, is more successful than one might expect. In her unpublished memoirs Johnston said the inspiration for the character came from the Lucy poem by Wordsworth which begins "Three years she grew in sun and shower." It is evident that Audrey was intended to be a simple child of nature, and throughout the novel she is seen against and associated with such a backdrop. Though devoting much space to descriptions of nature, Johnston emphasizes the human drama; she uses nature primarily to help establish that Audrey is unsophisticated, naive, direct, honest, incapable of guile herself or of recognizing it in others. The portrait is very much in keeping with the conventional stereotype of female virtue expected in heroines of sentimental novels. To make Audrey exceptional, Johnston gives her qualities which are not merely natural; she acquires the supernatural aura of folklore, legend, and myth. To Haward she seems an elf or wood sprite, a "dryad" (112) who lives in a beech tree; to the reader, her story awakens echoes of Cinderella and Pygmalion, and there are at least two allusions to Audrey as Eloisa. It is sometimes difficult to recall that she began as the simple child of English pioneers in the mountains when she finally discovers "her heritage of art" (275) and becomes a great success as an actress. Even reviewers otherwise persuaded by her portrait found that success "a mere cliché"[26] and "the one real flaw in the story."[27]

If the portrait of Audrey strains all laws of probability, it does so in the interest of creating a truly memorable heroine, and it succeeds in that respect.

The portrait of her benefactor is equally memorable and successful, but for quite different reasons. Marmaduke Haward is one of the most complex, and therefore most interesting, of Johnston's literary creations. His good intentions, mixed with selfishness, and his generous but ineffectual, indecisive actions mark him as more credibly human than the idealized and stereotyped heroes or villains of conventional romance. Johnston's analysis of the specific nature of his flaws and motives reveals a depth of insight which makes the portrait more than a modest success. His flaws seem, on one level, to be merely the result of his being a man "of his time, and its laxness of principle and conduct; if he held within himself the potential scholar, statesman, and philosopher, there were also the skeptic, the egotist, and the libertine" (28). One soon learns that these contradictory impulses have led to a deeper flaw; Haward himself is unable to decide which of the various persons he is or wishes to become. His indecisiveness, in turn, leads to flaws which affect others; he develops a coldness, a detachment, which isolates him from other persons, and he learns to pose, to wear masks, to play roles in his dealings with other people. Unfortunately, his isolation from persons who are governed by feelings leads to some miscalculations about roles he should play.

Part of the success of the portrait is that it is revealed in action rather than authorial comments. Johnston shows in scenes with MacLean that Haward has returned from London sophisticated but bored. Having consciously pursued worldly pleasures, he believes life has little to offer, and he values it little. The remarkable scene in which Haward offers Evelyn a marriage of convenience dramatically reveals his flaws; he is too cold to comprehend that she feels the love he says does not exist between them, and his reaction to her refusal is revealing; he sees it as a temporary blunder which can be remedied. Miss Johnston says "the profound indifferentism of his nature enabled him to view the ruins with composure" (65).

His most serious blunder is his attempt to make Audrey over according to his wishes. From the very beginning his motives are mixed and his actions questionable. Resolving impulsively to make her a lady, "his own benevolence warmed his heart" (36), but he fails to follow through on his scheme. After discovering the natural flower she has become despite his neglect, he gradually persuades himself that he should renew his aid. Two kinds of love result; hers is the simple, innocent worship of her protector, but his is neither simple nor innocent. He plays the role of romantic lover in his imagination, calling her his Eloisa and writing poetry, but he is quite soberly aware that a marriage would be socially impossible. His ambivalent feelings and actions precipitate the major crisis of the novel: Haward alone fails to see how much harm results from his willful insistence that the lady he has created appear at the governor's ball. His motives and actions throughout make him more comprehensible to a modern audience, of course, than most idealized heroes or villains of the Romance of Adventure; one must agree with the contemporary reviewer who admired the novel as a "study in temperamental psychology."[28]

Most reviews of *Audrey* were fair and accurate in describing the novel's strengths and weaknesses. Typical were the reviewers who acknowledged the excesses of the Romance of Adventure but credited Johnston with being the most successful creator of the type.[29] In light of its evocation of an especially interesting aspect of colonial Virginia's history and its depth of character analysis, *Audrey* indeed "deserves more than a fleeting day of fame."[30]

IV Sir Mortimer *(1904)*

After the promise of Johnston's earlier novels, *Sir Mortimer* is a disappointment. It is based upon an idea which seems to have great potential, the story of an Elizabethan sea captain, an adventurer whose exploits supposedly are unknown only because overshadowed by those of Drake, Frobisher, and Hawkins. The novel suffers, however, from a confusion of design and lack of development. Many of the qualities which distinguished Johnston's earlier novels from the superficial popular historical romances of the day are only faintly present in *Sir Mortimer*.

The story begins in the late sixteenth century as a group of adventurers prepare to set sail in pursuit of fame and fortune. Sir Mortimer Ferne, who writes verses in the manner of his friend Sir Philip Sidney, hopes to bring honor to his "Dione," the Mistress Damaris Sedley, and to refute the insinuations of cowardice made by his jealous rival, Sir Robert Baldry. Ferne incurs further envy when he rescues Baldry during a storm and captures a Spanish ship. Ferne's fortunes turn after capturing the town, but not the fortress, at Nueva Cordoba; the wily Luiz de Guardiola, having captured Ferne, leads his attempted rescuers into a trap, capturing Baldry and burning Ferne's ship. Luiz releases Ferne with the report that he is responsible for the disaster, having given away the plans under torture. Ferne lives in self-acknowledged disgrace, spurning the consolations of friends and his loved one. His disgrace deepens when, setting out at last to make amends, he learns Baldry has been burned by the Spanish. His ship lost in Panama, he ministers to the Indians for three years. Reappearing disguised as a friar, he is repentant for having let revenge rule his life. He recovers fame and love, however, when one of Luiz's lieutenants reveals Ferne's presumed treachery was a fiction created to torment him.

The story as originally conceived offered many opportunities for melodramatic excitement, and the lines of conflict are well established early in the novel. One expects an Elizabethan adventurer with a jealous rival to struggle through various battles and hardships, some caused by the rival's schemes, and eventually perhaps to meet the rival in direct combat. However, there are few battles—Johnston passes over the "downright sinking of a small fleet from Hispaniola"[31] in a paragraph—and no real struggles with Baldry; midway through the novel he is replaced as antagonist when the conflict becomes Ferne's self-proclaimed disgrace, and the story struggles on thereafter without benefit of exciting incidents. Even dramatic struggles with nature, so prominent in many of Johnston's novels, are not developed to their full potential; the storm which sinks Baldry's ship is called "a maniac unchained" (51) but is not described. One's impression is that Johnston changed her mind about writing a Romance of Adventure before the novel was finished.

The latter half of the novel is more comprehensible as a story of internal character conflict, a study of the effects of guilt upon a man with an almost fanatic sense of honor, but even as such it suffers from confusion and inconsistency. A reviewer remarked about the improbability that Ferne's confession of guilt would be taken seriously, since he was obviously delirious;[32] equally improbable is his setting off upon more adventures to assuage his guilt, and the reversal of fortunes at the end undercuts whatever interest one may have developed in his internal drama. To show his hardships as entirely the fault of others is to argue that Ferne is without flaws; that idealization is both ineffective and inconsistent.

While Ferne's character is inconsistently developed, the other characters and the historical background are underdeveloped. The maid of honor Damaris is a stereotyped ideal of feminine beauty and loyalty, and Luiz's cruelty and deceit are assumed to follow from his being a Spaniard. In *Sir Mortimer* Johnston is guilty of using historical characters in the strained, improbable manner of her contemporaries. The report that Edmund Spenser would like for Ferne to complete his " 'old scheme which he forsook of King Arthur and his Knights' " (222) is the worst of several examples. The only extended effort to fill out the historical context occurs in Johnston's attempts to reproduce the "courtly affectation of similes run mad" (36). She says Damaris "could parley euphuism with the best" (35) and attempts to prove it with examples. The dialogue of the novel resembles, however, the stilted language of popular romance more than the language of Elizabethan England.

Most features of the novel so resemble the undistinguished efforts of Johnston's contemporaries that one might assume conscious imitation if the circumstances of writing did not offer a better explanation. The editors of *Harper's*, hoping to take advantage of her popular success, requested that she give them a short story; the project grew to be a novel stretching over twelve installments. The writing was a more arduous task than Johnston, ill at the time, was prepared to undertake. Although *Sir Mortimer* was a modest popular and financial success, it pleased neither Johnston nor her reviewers very much; the majority of the reviews were unfavorable.

Even if personal circumstances had not made it impossible for Johnston to give her best efforts to *Sir Mortimer*, it probably would not have measured up to her earlier historical romances, because she shows evidence of having begun to lose interest in the genre— just as its popularity with the general public was fading as well. Her father's death and her own continuing illness caused her to put aside fiction entirely for almost four years, and when she took it up again it was to write works markedly different from her first efforts.

V The Goddess of Reason *(1907)*

By Miss Johnston's own account in her diary begun in 1908, *The Goddess of Reason* was the "work of a mind just recovering its equilibrium" during the period of grief and convalescence following her father's death and her own serious illness. She had continued to postpone work on *Lewis Rand* (1908) because "every association with it was painful," turning instead to an "idea of a play of the French Revolution" which had lain dormant since her youth. The play which resulted suggests neither that Johnston's idea had improved with maturity nor that she had fully recovered her powers as a writer. Whether her source of inspiration lay in the kind of plays which served as vehicles for Audrey's display of histrionic talent or in the popular theatrics of Johnston's own day, she created a thoroughly sentimental melodrama. *The Goddess of Reason* was the only play Johnston completed, and little about it indicates that her later decison not to carry through with other projected plays was a mistake.

The Goddess of Reason is a blank-verse drama in five acts set in France during the years 1791-1794; specific political conflicts of the developing revolution form the backdrop for the timeless, primary conflicts of love and honor. The protagonist is the beautiful young peasant girl Yvette, who is of aristocratic lineage but does not know it; she loves and is loved by the Baron René-Amaury De Vardes, who is her protector but also a representative of the aristocracy her own class wishes to overthrow. Specific antagonists are another peasant girl, Angélique, who is jealous of Yvette, and De Vardes's childhood friend, Rémond Lalain, a Jacobin opportunist.

The play opens on the morning after an attack by "sansculottes and tatterdemalions,"[33] led by Yvette, upon the home of De Vardes, an aristocrat who nevertheless has sympathy for the "misguided" peasants (21). His frivolous friends feel secure, especially after the culprits are apprehended, and are disappointed that De Vardes releases the peasants with only a warning. Exposition in Act I also establishes Yvette's origins and De Vardes's love for her. Act II finds Yvette torn between De Vardes, who has installed her in a convent while he goes to fight for the king, and her loyalties to her class; others taunt her for being kept by an aristocrat, report that De Vardes actually loves the Marquise De Blanchefôret, and urge her to rejoin the struggle because Angélique is supplanting her as leader. Act III opens in 1794 with the revolution triumphant and Yvette celebrated as the Goddess of Reason. She convinces the mob to spare De Vardes, but when he pleads mercy for the Marquise, Yvette is enraged and denounces both. Act IV features scenes of pathos as aristocrats prepare for death. Yvette learns too late that she has been deceived about the friendship of De Vardes and the Marquise; she has spent the night with Lalain to secure their release but discovers the Marquise is already dead. In Scene 1 of Act V De Vardes is condemned and Yvette denounces Lalain and the republic. Herself denounced, in Scene 2 Yvette and De Vardes affirm their love as both prepare to be drowned in the Loire.

Though some of her earlier works had been dramatized, Johnston did not succeed in her attempt to adapt features of her Romances of Adventure directly for the stage. By its nature the dramatic medium emphasized some of the least successful aspects of her early work. Unrelieved pathos is the tone throughout, an excess of sentimentality not as objectionable in the novels, and no complexity or subtlety is introduced to compensate for Johnston's tendency to stereotype characters. Her difficulties with plot construction are painfully evident; even though the scope of the action is not so broad as in the novels, the audience's imagination would be severely tested to fill gaps in the sequence of events. As the reviewer of a performance noted, "It is no easy matter to take an epoch and make it fit into a five-act play."[34] Realistic dialogue never had been one of Johnston's strengths, and having to write a work which consisted entirely of dialogue placed her at a great disadvantage. To present the dialogue in blank verse was perhaps not entirely inappropriate, but the quality was in one reviewer's opinion "mediocre" and at times "intolerable."[35] The New York Times drama critic objected to the "abominable practice"[36] of using French phrases and the substitution of long speeches for action. Every line seems to be a struggle for new heights of eloquence, every speech a declamation; some are effective, such as Yvette's enumeration of hardships as she calculates her age, but more typical is Yvette's lament "oh, woe is me!" (184).

Not only were Johnston's faults highlighted by the dramatic medium, but also some of the qualities which distinguished her Romances of Adventure from those of her contemporaries were lost. The Goddess of Reason certainly does not realize the potential complexity of the conflicts. The audience is aware that De Vardes and Yvette are victimized by the partisan atmosphere of the time, but Yvette's error is more the result of simple jealousy than revolutionary zeal; the play focuses upon the personal problems of the characters and neglects the larger issues. Nor did drama allow Johnston to make use of her skill in realizing the natural setting and relating it to thematic concerns. Deprived of the opportunity to comment directly, Johnston at the beginning of each act provided stage directions in an attempt to evoke the setting, but they are a poor substitute for passages in her novels; moreover, such items as "sea beating against a dangerous coast" (1) would have been impossible to represent adequately in performance.

Reviews of the published version varied, but they identified enough problems to make questionable the play's potential for successful performance. An instructive message was provided by the reviewer who called it "the most *readable* poetic drama . . . that has lately been seen."[37] Despite its disadvantages, however, *The Goddess of Reason* was brought to the stage by Julia Marlowe, an actress noted for her portrayal of Shakespearean and romantic roles. Her reputation, and perhaps Johnston's, helped make the first performance in Boston on December 21, 1908, a newsworthy occasion; as the *New York Times* reported, "the audience was a notable one, leading State officials and representatives of Harvard University occupying boxes."[38] The critical reception of the play when it moved to New York in February 1901 was not as enthusiastic. A *Times* reviewer found the play "neither impressive as poetry or drama"[39] and, while recognizing the role of Yvette as a choice one for displaying Julia Marlowe's talents, regretted that she had wasted her talents on it. No doubt the high points of the play were Miss Marlowe's scenes calculated to evoke tears and the spectacular parade scene, featuring busts of Voltaire, Rousseau, Franklin, and Robespierre, a miniature guillotine, and Yvette, "a radiant picture borne aloft on the triumphal car."[40] Reliance upon tears and spectacle in the performance, of course, confirms that *The Goddess of Reason* has little intrinsic merit as drama.

The work was neither a popular nor a critical success, and it may have been a valuable lesson to Johnston about what she should not attempt; more important, it helped free her to return to the work she had so long postponed.

CHAPTER 3

Historical Novels

D URING the five years following publication of her verse drama, Johnston completed three novels that had been developing for some time. *Lewis Rand, The Long Roll,* and *Cease Firing* were the most ambitious works she had attempted, and in the context of her whole career they are, for varying reasons, her most significant and best works. The latter two focus upon the Civil War, and their most perceptive analyst has said they "may be taken as one work."[1] Another writer has argued that all three constitute "a trilogy in that they contain the history of one Albemarle County family, the Carys, from Jefferson's time to the fall of the Confederacy."[2] Both views need qualification, because the works differ substantially in subject and tone. Yet they clearly are a unit and mark a new phase in Johnston's career.

All three originated in Johnston's sense of obligation to her family and region. The idea for *Lewis Rand* occurred to her soon after she had completed *Audrey,* and it undoubtedly was nourished by conversations with her father about events of the century which had just ended.[3] Realizing that her health would not allow her to undertake the quantity of research necessary to write the novel, she put it aside for easier work. Her father's death deprived her of a valuable resource but ultimately was the motivating force that led her to complete the book as a memorial. Similarly, the Civil War novels proceeded from a sense of loyalty to her family and region. Johnston wished not only to honor the memory of her father, from whom she had learned much in spite of his reluctance to discuss his own war experiences, but also the social order and intellectual concept for which he had fought. Specific impetus was provided by an invitation to speak at Vicksburg during the dedication of a memorial to the Botetourt County artillery unit with which her father had served. She attended the ceremony in November 1907 and listened as a "Gen. Lee" read the address she had prepared. The qualities of heroism described in the remarks were those she would soon attempt to dramatize.[4]

The writing was in each case a long, painful, arduous task. Each novel required extensive research and evoked disturbing memories; the task was sometimes tedious and often intellectually demanding. Grief, illness, and travel delayed the completion of *Lewis Rand*, which went through several title changes, until July 1908; later, a developing involvement with suffrage work and other causes complicated a task the completion of which demonstrated a special sense of dedication.

Most importantly, the seriousness of purpose which lay behind the works is paralleled by a change in their character. The merits which distinguished Johnston's best Romances of Adventure were heightened; she created a greater impression of historical accuracy, explored more significant ideas, and in some cases provided deeper probing of character. Some changes are more than a matter of degree; events depicted are less a loose chain of coincidence than a pattern of inevitable consequences, and the works contain a wide range of tones, some much more complicated than the sentimentality or pathos of melodrama. When compared to Johnston's Romances of Adventure, the novels are, in most senses of the word, more realistic and better fit Leisy's characterization of the "historical novel proper," which "shows respect for historical fiction as an art"[5] and rests upon a "valid hypothesis of human nature, regardless of locale."[6] At the same time, as Lawrence G. Nelson has argued, they may best be understood within the context of "Shakespearean tragedy"[7] and epic literature.[8] In short, they represent a complex and substantial achievement with merits difficult to explain within conventional categories of analysis.

I Lewis Rand *(1908)*

Lewis Rand reveals a significant shift in Mary Johnston's interests toward more serious subject matter and a more realistic form. While retaining some elements of the Romance of Adventure which had established her popularity, she develops in this novel an extended study of obsessive ambition and pride nourished by a time which fostered opportunism. It is the story of a self-made man who wishes to become a king and whose ambition, given the example of Napoleon, the encouragement of Aaron Burr, and the enormous potential of the unconquered regions in the West, was not so improbable as it may now seem. Johnston vividly shows that the infant American republic was in jeopardy during the early years of the nineteenth century, and her portrait is convincing because it is developed within the framework of the story of one man.

Two introductory chapters show Lewis Rand at age fourteen, even this young driven by an ambition to rise in the world but frustrated because his father, a tobacco-roller and horse tamer, is determined that he remain ignorant. Through the intervention of Thomas Jefferson, Rand is allowed to study law, and, by 1804, at age twenty-eight, he has become more than Jefferson's protégé; he wins election to the Virginia House of Delegates as the Democrat-Republican candidate, defeating the Federalist Ludwell Cary, whom he has envied since youth. Rand tells the frontiersman Adam Gaudylock that the victory is not satisfying; he longs to see the West. Accidentally thrown from his horse, Rand is cared for at the home of Colonel Richard and Major Edward Churchill, friends of the Carys and uncles of Jacqueline Churchill; the Churchill family is distressed when Jacqueline refuses Ludwell Cary's proposal and outraged when Rand takes advantage of his opportunity to declare the love he has for years felt for Jacqueline. They marry just before news arrives that Aaron Burr has killed Alexander Hamilton and gone into hiding. The marriage and Rand's fortunes prosper, but he breaks with Jefferson over the issue of whether to create new states in the Louisiana Territory and secretly becomes involved with Burr's scheme to create a kingdom in the West. Cary suspects his involvement and publishes a letter about unbridled ambition which Rand chooses to take personally. Major Churchill, hoping to protect Jacqueline, unsuccessfully urges Rand to run for governor so that he will have to remain in Virginia. Rand suspects Cary's influence and challenges him to a duel, which Cary postpones long enough to prevent the Rands' departure for the West. Rand is infuriated when Cary only fires in the air, and he feels no gratitude when Burr's plot is discovered before he is publicly involved. Overtaking Cary by chance on the secluded river road between Charlottesville and Richmond, Rand accuses him of trying to use his barely avoided disgrace to alienate Jacqueline, and, further enraged by Cary's "restraint,"[9] Rand kills him. Covering his tracks, he is unrepentant and astonished that Jacqueline, who will not desert him despite her sorrow, thinks he should confess. The Churchills suspect Rand of the murder but have no proof and do not wish to involve Jacqueline. Cary's brother Fairfax sets out to find evidence and gradually pieces together enough to confront Rand with the choice of confessing or being accused. By this time suffering remorse and aware of the magnitude of his crimes, Rand chooses to confess and face imprisonment.

The development of Rand's story shows a considerable gain in Johnston's ability to construct a well-unified plot. Only the device of having Rand seen by the dancing master as he emerges from the woods after killing Cary is implausible in a plot neither excessively episodic nor heavily dependent upon coincidence. The structure consists of a series of climaxes—Rand's marriage, the duel, revelation of Burr's conspiracy, the murder, and the confession—but most of the incidents of the plot are logically unified and maintain an intensity of interest without resorting to the artificial excitement of melodrama. Even the duel scene is restrained in a way which shows Johnston more concerned with revelation of character than with creating excitement. Some reviewers questioned whether Rand's confession is adequately motivated or explained,[10] but that objection may be overcome by consideration of what Johnston developed as the principal conflict in the novel.

That conflict is a restless struggle within Rand to understand himself and to make peace with the forces driving him. Johnston skillfully integrates the private turmoil and his public involvement with politics. The lines of personal conflict are established early as Rand tells Adam Gaudylock he would rather be king in the West than governor in Virginia and will not hesitate to destroy anyone who stands in his way. The scene is one of several foreshadowing incidents which follow. One especially effective instance occurs on election day as Rand and Cary discuss their first meeting in the woods as boys. Agreeing they could not have foreseen their present circumstances, Cary says they, of course, also cannot foresee the last meeting and then offers a toast " 'To another meeting, in the wood!' " (51). What Cary represents becomes for Rand both the chief obstacle and main goal in his pursuit of success and happiness; he soon discovers that the marriage to Jacqueline does not end his resentment of Cary

While their personal rivalry takes precedence in the plot, their opposing ideologies expand the conflict into public affairs. The two embody signs of a change in the American social and political order that goes deeper than mere partisan politics, intense as that conflict between Federalist and Republican may have been. Cary stands for the old order of aristocratic values, of privilege, of genteel and chivalrous manners; Rand represents the common man who may rise through ability. While the successive stages of his rise to wealth, fame, and position suggest a tacit endorsement of the Jeffersonian principles he espouses, Johnston shows that Cary also is admirable and, for Lewis, enviable; the book is not critical of the principles of either side of the conflict, but rather of Rand's violation of his own principles.

Their conflict deepens because Rand is not content with personal or partisan victories. Cary accepts his losses with graceful and generous congratulations, and in his behavior Rand perceives a superiority he can never match by ordinary efforts. His sense that his real inferiority to Cary lies in his mean-spirited envy is confirmed by his feelings after Cary prevents his exposure as a traitor. What began as a desire to overcome the inferior social standing of his father becomes a destructive rage which is partially self-hatred. Rand willfully and pridefully rejects magnanimity, and his motives are best explained by Major Churchill's characterization of him as "arrogant as Lucifer" (307). Locked deep in the prison of his pride, a pride which like Lucifer's refuses redemption, Rand murders Cary; ironically, the murder does indeed bring release, redemption, and atonement. It deprives Rand of the focus for his rage, and he must turn inward for an explanation for his restlessness. He learns that the way to inner peace is not through conflict, even if one triumphs, and he learns that he must renounce all that he fought for, saving only Jacqueline's love, in order to find what he really wants. And so the ending of the novel seems reasonably consistent with the story Johnston develops; it is not the tragedy, but the reconciliation, which interested her.

Rand's story is thus an interesting variation on the theme of excess ambition, and it also is the first appearance in Mary Johnston's fiction of a theme that she later treated often, but perhaps never again so well—the amelioration of human conflict.[11] Her developing interest in the theme of reconciliation helps account for certain features of the characters Cary and Jacqueline, who also anticipate her later work. They are the most idealized characters in the novel and may seem to be quite unconvincing; however, the nature of their idealization is different from that of conventional stereotypes. Johnston emphasizes the qualities of tolerance and forgiveness; Jacqueline's refusal to desert Rand is almost incomprehensible except as a manifestation of a love and understanding which goes beyond that of ordinary human nature. It is very similar to the kind of behavior for which Mary Johnston became an advocate and which defines the characters in her later novels. Cary

and Jacqueline could be moved to her later novels without notice-
able inconsistencies, but their portraits succeed best in *Lewis Rand*
because they do not depend upon the intervention of mystical
insights to provide motivation.

Other fictional characters in the novel, while overshadowed by
Rand, are moderately well drawn, even though their portraits seem
intended as types. Colonel Dick is genial but ineffectual, incapable
of understanding why the Lewis Rands of the world would wish to
interfere with his comforts. Major Edward understands and is bitter;
he reads Swift and expects the worst in human nature. Tom Mocket,
Rand's assistant, is the prototype of the political henchman whose
loyalty is to a man, not to principles. Adam Gaudylock represents
the sturdy frontiersman whose interest in settling the West rises
above political machinations.

Johnston's handling of the historical characters is especially
interesting. Jefferson and Burr are crucial to the action, but for the
most part they remain as shadowy, almost allegorical background
figures. Jefferson personifies goodness betrayed, while Burr has a
demonic, threatening quality; an index to Rand's corruption is to be
seen in Burr's fear of what he may have created. Both are portrayed
with appropriate restraint; only the introduction of various specta-
tors such as Washington Irving at Burr's trial, even if historically
accurate, seems gratuitous.

Historical accuracy had been in the Romances of Adventure and
remained in *Lewis Rand* an important consideration for Mary
Johnston. Her research and many hours of discussions with her
father allowed her to portray the social and political context in
detail. Details of the geography of Charlottesville and Albemarle
County and the social customs of early nineteenth-century Virginia
provide a vivid sense of the place and time. The novel is especially
good in portraying the passionately intense politics of the day. Rand
and Cary maintain an appearance of gentlemanly decorum on
election day, but the biting and gouging during fights between their
followers perhaps more accurately represent the mood of partisan
politics. Several subtle details demonstrate that the aristocratic
Churchill and Cary families, while admirable, are out of touch with
the realities of their day. One of the significant successes of the
novel is that Johnston was able to draw a convincing picture of
historical characters and a historical setting without letting the
material overshadow the main plot.

Another success is the consistency of tone. One reviewer called the novel "sombre and grim,"[12] and only such vestiges of sentimentality as the character Vinnie, Tom Mocket's lisping sister, are preserved from Johnston's Romances of Adventure. The novel is certainly neither a conventional love story nor a melodramatic novel of action; rather, it is an appropriately restrained but intense portrayal of a struggle which has overtones of tragedy and a reconciliation without cheer. It may have disappointed readers who expected another Romance of Adventure, but it pleased many readers, too.

It was, in fact, both a popular and a critical success. Contemporary reviewers recognized and praised what they perceived to be substantial gains; one said it was "notable for a deepening of thought and a maturity of analysis that are almost startling in comparison with its predecessors,"[13] and another predicted it would "add to her reputation as a serious novelist."[14] The *New York Times* reviewer called it "one of the strongest works of fiction that has seen the light of day in America."[15] This high praise unfortunately has been diminished in the comments of literary historians. Ernest Leisy praises its "psychological approach to character" but misrepresents the difference between Johnston's Romances of Adventure and *Lewis Rand* by calling it "a picture of a feudal society on mimosa-scented plantations, with soft-voiced darkies singing in the moonlight, and an occasional conflict between neighbors and hotheaded sons."[16]

Lewis Rand is, by the customary measures of literary criticism, Mary Johnston's most successful novel. Though it retains some features of her Romances of Adventure, it uses a well-constructed plot, plausible characters, a consistent tone, and a fully developed context to treat absorbing personal and public conflicts with seriousness and insight. Only the two novels which followed can compete with *Lewis Rand* for significance within the context of Johnston's career, and that significance lies in qualities other than their merits as fiction. If it does not match the aesthetic accomplishments of the very best American novelists, *Lewis Rand* is nevertheless an accomplishment of sufficient merit to need no apologies. Literary critics and historians owe Johnston and themselves the favor of reexamination.

II   The Long Roll (1911)

The Long Roll was Mary Johnston's most ambitious undertaking, and, if the result is not the masterpiece which some early readers called it, it is nevertheless the high point of her career. Planned as the first volume of a trilogy dealing with the War Between the States, *The Long Roll* is set in Virginia during the years 1860 to 1863, from the outset of the war to the death of General Thomas Henry "Stonewall" Jackson. It was intended to be an apology, in the original meaning of the word, for the Southern Cause. Begun by Johnston out of a sense of duty to the memory of her father and loyalty to her region, it argues that the war was fought nobly, not in defense of slavery but in defense of an idea. During the writing the subject became a much more elaborate study of military tactics and the effects of war upon individuals and groups. It succeeds in ways not matched by any of her other works because it deals with profound conflicts on a grand scale, where more than the fortunes of individuals are at stake, and also dramatizes the human consequences of such events.

The Long Roll contains three main lines of development, not equally successful but moderately well integrated into a complex whole. The first involves a set of fictional characters centered upon Richard Cleave, Judith Cary, and Maury Stafford, Cleave's rival in both war and love. The second concerns progress of the war itself and includes detailed descriptions of battles, forced marches, and leaders of the Confederacy. The developing stature of one of these leaders, "Stonewall" Jackson, forms the third line of development and the only one completed within the book; Johnston's portrait of Jackson was the most controversial aspect of *The Long Roll*, but it provides an internal unity and becomes perhaps the most significant accomplishment of the novel.

The book opens with the reading of the "Botetourt Resolutions" and the reactions of both prominent and obscure people to the possible coming of war. The prevailing sentiment is that reconciliation is desirable, but not at the expense of violating the covenant of states' rights to secede from the union. Richard Cleave correctly predicts not only that war will come but also the precise difficulties which eventually cause the war to be lost. His judgment about his relations with Judith is not so wise; he leaves without seeing her because he mistakenly thinks she prefers Stafford.

Excitement and hope prevail among all social classes as the war begins but fade rapidly when the realities of combat and the hardships of forced marches are encountered. Jackson begins to command respect despite his eccentricities when his ability to make soldiers out of unprepared civilians and his tactics of evasion and surprise bring victories. The carnival atmosphere at the first battle

of Manassas quickly changes to panic and horror, and both sides
recognize that the struggle will not end quickly. Winter conditions
in the mountains bring "a side of war which Walter Scott had never
painted,"[17] and some troops grumble about Jackson's pushing.
Quarreling with Cleave, Stafford calls Jackson a " 'diseased mind—
a Presbyterian deacon crazed for personal distinction' " (166).
Cleave is disciplined by Jackson for failing to reveal the nature of
Stafford's insult. A brief respite in the fighting allows Cleave to visit
Judith and learn that Stafford has lied, and that she loves him, not
Stafford; confronting Stafford with the information, Cleave makes
an enemy who promises revenge.

Jackson's clever tactics in defending Staunton help bolster defen-
ses in the West, but in the East the news is bad. Richmond is
threatened by McClellan, General Johnston is wounded, and the
gallant Colonel Ashby is killed. Lee assumes command in the East,
and Jackson promises to help as events progress toward the battle of
the Seven Days. Many of the events are reported from the perspective of the cowardly deserter Steven Dagg, whose drunken incom-
petence and lies also get Cleave into deep trouble. Jackson, myste-
riously not himself for a time, withdraws from the battle, and
Cleave, sent a wrong order by Stafford, leads the Stonewall Brigade
to destruction. Dismissed from the army, Cleave refuses to marry
Judith while in disgrace and disappears, only to rejoin the artillery
disguised as the mountain man Philip Deaderick. The fighting and
the troops become more primitive as the war seems to be stalemated,
but builds to another climax at the Battle of the Wilderness. On the
eve of battle, Jackson, recognizing Cleave, questions him and
promises a court of inquiry if Stafford, now a prisoner, returns. After
routing Federal troops toward Chancellorsville, however, Jackson is
wounded by his own troops when mistaken for a Yankee cavalry-
man. His death several days later and heroic funeral bring the book
to a close, but the conclusion clearly looks forward to Gettysburg.
Passing in review of Jackson's remains, the schoolmaster Allan Gold
reflects that the Confederacy must follow Jackson's frequent admo-
nition to " *'Press forward!'* " (682).

A.   *The Fictional Element*

Least successful of the three lines of development in the book is
that which uses the fictional characters. The principal characters of
the love triangle and their conflicts seem out of place in a work

which depends heavily upon realism for its effects. While Johnston probably hoped to suggest that Cleave's idealistic and courtly behavior was typical of the Southern aristocrat-warrior, and while she no doubt intended that Judith would epitomize the long-suffering endurance of Southern women, both portraits seem more typical of characters in romance. Stafford's unbridled ambition and determination to have Judith at any cost remind one of similar qualities in Lewis Rand, but his motives are never as well developed; a reader unfamiliar with Rand would dismiss Stafford as a rather conventional romantic antagonist. The conflicts among the three are woven into the novel with some skill; though Johnston has to strain probability somewhat to bring the men together with Jackson at so many critical stages, one's main objection is that their conflicts never achieve the intensity or significance of the larger conflicts.

Since several members of Judith's family were characters or are descended from characters in *Lewis Rand,* one is led to search for some special purpose for focusing upon the Cary family; but only the fact that they have aristocratic origins and ties to the Union is important to the novel. The Carys seem included as a convenience rather than a necessity. Johnston wished to show the effects of war upon all social classes, and the Carys are representative of a class that had much to lose.

Some minor characters, such as the schoolmaster Allan Gold and the mountain man Billy Maydew, while also idealized as types of their station in life, are both more human and more effectively used to dramatize the larger issues of the book. Their direct involvement in and responses to the horrors of war, and their varying degrees of comprehension of the significance of events, show the effects of war in a vivid and meaningful way. Throughout the book appears an assortment of minor characters based upon real persons, and, if not well developed, they are nevertheless credible; the incidents involving them convincingly display the ravages of war.

Johnston's most successful fictional portrait is of the least attractive character, Steven Dagg. She explores in considerable detail the motives of his cowardice and the incidents in which he tries to leave the war or change sides. He is representative of a social class which had little to gain or lose from the conflict, but more importantly he is shown to be representative of a side of human nature; he has no principles to defend, is mainly concerned about his safety and comfort, and has been caught up in a conflict he does not understand. Johnston's honesty in showing through Steven Dagg that not all soldiers are heroic and her care in developing the portrait to some extent balance any excess of romance in her treatment of the fictional characters of *The Long Roll*.

B. *The War*

Both more realistic and more successful is her development of the second major element of the book, the progress of the war itself.

Mary Johnston was well prepared by the experiences of her own life and by extensive research when she undertook the task of representing the war. As soon as *Lewis Rand* was finished she began a program of reading to prepare her for a volume, tentatively entitled "War," which would not only memorialize her father but vindicate the actions of her cousin, General Joseph Eggleston Johnston, and for that matter the South itself. There was no dearth of material to inspect; her diaries record the reading of such works as Alexander Stephens's *War Between the States*, Major Robert Stiles's *Four Years Under Marse Robert*, her cousin's *Narrative of Military Operations*, Mrs. Mary Boykin Chesnut's *Diary From Dixie*, "thirty volumes Southern Historical Society papers,"[18] and Lt.-Col. G. F. R. Henderson's two-volume *Stonewall Jackson and the American Civil War*. The work progressed slowly and required much rereading. By May 1909, her plan had crystallized as "not one volume but three—a trilogy." Meeting resistance from her publishers, who feared that her plan and subject matter would not be well received, she persisted until *The Long Roll* was completed in March 1911; her only concession was to collapse the second and third volumes into one novel, *Cease Firing*, published in 1912.

Fears about reception of the subject matter were moderately well grounded. Only a few thought her viewpoint slanted, but several reviewers objected that the book was more history than fiction. Almost without exception her treatment of the war has been praised for its accuracy and thoroughness, the consensus being much like the opinion of Louis D. Rubin, Jr., that the novels are "justly praised for their fidelity to detail, their intimate presentation of Confederate operations both from command and rear rank."[19] Unfortunately, many readers also have agreed with Rubin that these are the only virtues of the books, and some have doubted that they are virtues at all. One reviewer said *The Long Roll* was not a novel but "military history . . . devoid of the constructive art which might have made all these matters the accessories of a logically developed dramatic action."[20] Perhaps the reviewer has reacted to the romantic principal characters and overlooked the significance of the minor characters; certainly he ignores the constructive powers Johnston displayed in making the war dramatic. Not enough readers have noted both the general patterns and specific techniques used to make *The Long Roll* more than history.

The general pattern, of course, was bound by the limits of actual events, but within those limits Johnston was free to interpret what coherent design could be discovered in the chaos of war. The design is complex; it shows a civilization divided and seemingly pointed toward destruction but capable of evolving powers of endurance which bring heroism and a wiser sense of the need for reconciliation. The early stage shows both North and South with a pride bordering upon vanity and an innocence shading into ignorance. Federal officers could at that stage invite congressmen's wives to watch the battles, and Confederate troops marched off amidst a gala celebration with banners, bugles, and the fond farewells of women they expected to see again in a few weeks. In the battle scenes which follow, the soldiers progressively become more knowledgeable about the horrors of war and are transformed into more elemental human beings. They descend almost to the point of savagery when, their ammunition expended, they resort to throwing rocks in hand-to-hand combat that has become primitive and personal. Growing at the same time, however, is a sense of determination which ultimately produces the mutual respect out of which could be effected a reconciliation. Several scenes show that anger is transformed into admiration for the courage, and sympathy for the suffering, of opponents. Many readers called Johnston's treatment of the war epic, and it is clear that she had found a theme equal to the kind of treatment she elsewhere attempted to impose on lesser subjects. Her handling of the pattern of its development also justifies describing it, in Lawrence G. Nelson's phrase, as "symphonic, with complex contrapuntal effects throughout."[21]

Johnston's devices for developing the pattern deserve credit as demonstrations that her concept of the war included more than just battles and tactics. While much of the action is necessarily told from the panoramic view of the omniscient narrator, many events are given from the perspective of the participants; the episodes of Dagg's desertion are good examples, but so are the sequences which follow Allan Gold in battle and back home in the mountains. The scene dramatizing festivities surrounding the Confederate army's custom of electing its officers, featuring debates, singing, and a performance of Sheridan's *The Rivals* is an effective way to characterize the mood and life of the army at rest. The chapter entitled "The Ironclads"[22] shows the Cary family listening to a report of the fight of the *Merrimac* and *Monitor;* it helps dramatize the home front's anxiety and eagerness for news of the war. Conscious artistry is displayed, as Grant Overton pointed out years ago, in the scene of Jackson's funeral; the description of the funeral procession and the progression of mourners has both movement and a gradually narrowing focus.[23]

Jackson's funeral is a scene designed to evoke strong feelings, and it is only one of several charged with intense emotion. Johnston portrays a wide range of emotions, from comic relief through fear and grief to exaltation. No doubt she was able to rely upon the memories of her readers to aid in responding to the significance of many events, but her own skills contribute much. The pace and restraint of her treatment of such events as the Confederates' discovery of the effects of the "Rebel Yell" reveal a skill surpassing her handling of the emotions of the fictional lovers and rivals.

It should be evident that accuracy is not the only virtue of Johnston's handling of the war. Those readers who found the material tedious or irrelevant missed some qualities which well compensate any reader's patience in indulging her desire to be thorough. The third line of development adds a quality not supplied by the first two, a sense of completeness, and has other virtues as well.

C. *Jackson*

That *The Long Roll* would focus upon Jackson was a part of Johnston's original plan; a diary entry says of the planned trilogy that "the first would close with Chancellorsville—and Stonewall Jackson the dominant historical figure." Neither Joseph E. Johnston nor Lee, who were to be central in the second and third volumes, is treated as comprehensively or convincingly in the one volume she actually produced as the continuation of the saga. The portrait of Jackson dominates not just the historical element but the whole book. It shows a man with very human weaknesses but supremely fitted for the demands of his time and place, a man whose strengths and even weaknesses conspired with circumstances to make him heroic, a man whose accomplishments and stature made him the symbol for a cause.

The qualities emphasized in Johnston's portrait are a combination of eccentricities and genius. Jackson's peculiarities of manner and behavior are stressed early and often; he is "an awkward, inarticulate, and peculiar man" (60) who "sucked lemons for dyspepsia . . . rode a rawboned nag named Little Sorrel . . . carried his sabre in the oddest fashion, and said 'oblike' instead of 'oblique' " (61). His inflexible justice, lack of humor, supreme confidence in his own judgment (because he relies upon God's help), and unwillingness to discuss his plans do not endear him to his troops; they think he wants "an implicity of obedience which might have been in order with some great and glorious captain, some idolized Napoleon, but which seemed hardly the due of the late professor of natural philosophy and artillery tactics at the Virginia Military Institute" (61). It is conceded that he goes to great lengths to correct a mistake but rarely thinks that necessary. His dislike for swearing, his constant praying, and his reluctance to fight on Sunday make some think him a religious fanatic, and Stafford is not the only person who feels Jackson is driven by personal ambition.

However, the driving force is revealed to be not ambition but the same spirit of determination which by his example is gradually nourished in his troops. It is evidenced in his strategic and tactical genius but also in his regard for his troops. He drives them until they drop from exhaustion but holds up the whole army for a half hour while an old woman searches for her son to give him some socks. Describing Jackson's "inner self," Johnston says he was

indomitable, a thunderbolt of war, a close-mouthed, far-seeing, praying and worshipping, more or less ambitious, not always just, patriotically devoted fatalist and enthusiast, a mysterious and commanding genius of an iron sort. (144)

Johnston's analysis of his greatness defies conventional categories; she may best have indicated the impression she wished to convey when she called him an "awkward knight of the Holy Grail" (321).

The success of Johnston's portrait lies not only in the detailed development but also in its gradual revelation. There is little change in Jackson himself, but there is a definite pattern of development in the estimate given him. It is a pattern of discovery which reaches its

first crest when he becomes "Stonewall" Jackson at the Battle of
First Manassas but alternately recedes and crests throughout the
book. The low points are the occasions when he resigns after being
forced to retreat, his "fever" before the Battle of the Seven Days,
and the novel tactics which earn him the name "Fool Tom Jackson."
The gradual discovery of his genius leads ultimately to an apotheosis
which places him among Washington, Jefferson, and the great
military leaders of all ages. The tragic sense of loss felt by his
mourners and the resolution to continue the struggle are appropriate
both as climax and conclusion to the book, and they skillfully
foreshadow events to come.

D. Reactions

In spite of the stature accorded Jackson and the honesty and care
with which the portrait was constructed, Johnston's presentation
and analysis of Jackson's character sparked reactions among friends
and relatives of Jackson that flared into a controversy which
smoldered long after the main participants were dead.[24] Both the
facts and her interpretation of them were challenged by a writer
who felt that Johnston was wrong about Jackson's lack of humor
and not fair in representing his religious faith, and an article in the
Richmond Times-Dispatch summarized objections to the portrait
and other features of the book registered by various speakers at a
meeting of the Lee Camp of Confederate Veterans.[25] Johnston
replied with a letter to the same paper, arguing that Jackson's
greatness outweighed his faults, that an artist is required to be
honest, and that critics of her portrait were suggesting that she
should have ignored vast quantities of published sources that
demonstrate its accuracy.[26] Mrs. Jackson responded with a letter to
the New York Times which ended with a plea for "all true
Confederate soldiers" to protest if they agreed the portrait was
"false and damaging." She professed ignorance of some of the
details of the portrait, objected to implications that Jackson was not
of aristocratic descent, and took issue with the use of N. C. Wyeth's
"hideous caricature," rather than a real portrait, as frontispiece.[27]
Mrs. Jackson's most astonishing point is praise for the treatment of
Jackson in Henderson's book, because Johnston already had established that she had read Henderson five times. In light of her
extensive and meticulous research, objections to her factual accuracy
seem feeble and unconvincing.

The real issue, of course, is not the facts but what she did with them. One readily understands why those who wished to exalt Jackson were distressed by the emphasis upon his eccentricities, but it is precisely the mixture of eccentric and heroic qualities which makes the portrait credible, vital, and sympathetic. As one reviewer pointed out, Jackson is "the hero of the book, and he lives before us in something of the way in which Holbein, or Rembrandt, or Watts made men and women live in their canvas."[28] The disinterested reader finds Jackson's image suffers little, and the book gains greatly, from Johnston's decision to try to capture the real Jackson.

Johnston has not received in recent years sufficient credit for the significance of her accomplishment in *The Long Roll*. Certainly it received a great deal of attention when first published, and the praise in some reviews was lavish; one said it was written "with the vigor of a man, the vision of a poet, the sympathies of a woman and the accuracy of a scientist," comparing it with *The Iliad, The Aeneid, Paradise Lost*, and *The Divine Comedy*.[29] If the comment errs in its degree of praise, it at least avoids the error of those who attacked it as mere history or for having a plot "as negligible as the plot of the average musical comedy."[30] The most perceptive analysis of the work's significance is that portion of Lawrence G. Nelson's essay that develops the point made by several reviewers about the work's epic qualities. If Nelson neglects important differences between *The Long Roll* and *Cease Firing*, he nevertheless establishes convincingly that *The Long Roll* demands evaluation by a set of criteria different from those ordinarily applied to fiction. Unfortunately, his is the only essay which makes a serious attempt to discover what makes *The Long Roll*, if not Mary Johnston's best novel, her most significant work.

III   Cease Firing *(1912)*

That *Cease Firing* is the result of Johnston's plan to write two novels continuing the stories and issues developed in *The Long Roll* invites a comparison of the two. They share a common general purpose and subject: *Cease Firing* carries to a conclusion Johnston's treatment of the war and amplifies her justification of the Confederate cause. Continuity in the fictional plot is provided by development of the love triangle of the principal characters and presentation of the further misadventures of the laggard Stephen Dagg; again the treatment of the war features extensive descriptions and analyses of the tactics, strategies, and events of major battles and campaigns. However, while the two works have many features in common, they are substantially different in focus, scope, pace, and tone. The focus shifts to a new set of fictional characters, Edward Cary and Desiree Gaillard, and both the setting and cast of characters expand to encompass the war outside Virginia. As a result, the tempo is accelerated and the level of emotional intensity increases. The tone becomes both more partisan and more melancholy. If the differences are in degree rather than kind, they nevertheless combine to produce a novel both more conventional and more like Miss Johnston's Romances of Adventure.

Cease Firing opens in December 1862 near the flooded Mississippi River; among the Confederate soldiers bogged down is Edward Cary, brother of the heroine of *The Long Roll*. Falling instantly in love with and betrothed to the "awakened princess"[31] Desiree Gaillard while stranded at her plantation, soon to be swept away by the river, Edward departs to help defend Vicksburg. He learns that President Jefferson Davis has unwisely overruled General Joseph E. Johnston's desire to concentrate his troops to repel Grant's superior forces, and the siege begins. The scene switches to Virginia, where, despite the death of Jackson, hopes are high that one or two more successes will make the Union tire of the war, and then to the Northern prison where Maury Stafford is confined and undergoing a change of heart about his treatment of Richard Cleave. The scene then alternates between Vicksburg and Virginia as the war progresses toward the climactic turning points of the fall of Vicksburg and the battle of Gettysburg in early July 1863. The fortunes of both the Confederacy and individuals turn rapidly for the worse; inflation of currency and shortages of supplies compound the problems of equivocal leadership and questionable tactics as the South undergoes increasing hardship. The only positive note is that Stafford, exchanged for a Northern prisoner, makes a full confession and thus paves the way for Cleave to resume his identity and command. The Southern strategy becomes one of retreat and delay; the military action alternates between Virginia, where the successive battles of Spotsylvania, Cold Harbour, and Petersburg lead to the fall of Richmond, and eastern Tennessee, where Sherman launches his push through Atlanta to the sea. Desiree has joined Edward, who is with Johnston's troops attempting to delay Sherman; separated during the retreat into South Carolina, they are wounded by drunken Northern soldiers and find each other only to die together.

Cleave is "desperately wounded" (399) while unsuccessfully helping resist the pillage by Sheridan's troops in the Virginia mountains, but he recovers to marry Judith and seek out Stafford to offer friendship. The novel ends with the Army of Northern Virginia on its way to Appomattox.

That portion of the fictional plot which continues the conflict between Cleave and Stafford over Judith depends heavily upon readers' familiarity with events and motives explained in *The Long Roll*. The primary conflicts are not much developed because they have been, for the most part, resolved; Cleave and Judith have declared their love, and Cleave's reputation is well on the way to being restored when the novel opens. The main element in the conflict developed in *Cease Firing* is Stafford's own rehabilitation, which is said to be the result of changes effected by his year in prison. Neither the heightened perception which occurs when he faces hanging as a spy nor the miraculous coincidence of his being saved by a Northern officer he had helped earlier is very credible as explanation for his transformation, and his decision to make a full confession before General Lee and then to emulate Cleave's rejoining the army in the trenches does not seem probable.

If Stafford's behavior is inconsistent, then Cleave and Judith's suffers from the opposite defect; they are static characters who suffer from but are not changed by events. Their idealization as romantic types was one of the weaknesses of *The Long Roll*, but at least in that novel their roles were integral. In *Cease Firing* they are shadowy figures replaced as principal characters by the young lovers Edward and Desiree.

The introduction of Desiree and movement of Edward from the background to a leading role have the effect of adding a much more conventional love element to *Cease Firing*. While Johnston portrays Cleave and Judith as quiet, patient friends who can wait upon duty and honor, she shows Edward and Desiree as passionate lovers who allow no barriers of time or place to separate them. The intensity of their love and the sense that they are fated for each other add a quality of sentimental romance not stressed in *The Long Roll*, and the events chosen to display their heroic selflessness are easily predictable. If they are no more credible as human beings than their counterparts, they at least add melodramatic qualities in keeping with the tone Johnston sustained throughout the book. One senses that they were drawn to satisfy expectations of the reader of conventional love stories, that Johnston was less interested in them as characters than as vehicles to serve larger purposes. If so, they serve that purpose well, providing personal reactions to events in the war outside Virginia.

In this respect they fulfill the same purpose as Stephen Dagg, who, though not used as extensively as in *The Long Roll*, remains the best-drawn fictional character. The schoolmaster Allan Gold is infuriated by the news that Dagg, malingering at home in the mountains, has begun to court Christianna Maydew; before a subplot paralleling the principal characters' love triangle can develop, however, Christianna rejects Dagg as a coward. When fighting comes to the mountains, Dagg is forced back into action and becomes Johnston's witness to the wounding of Cleave and the destruction of the 65th Virginia Brigade. Having served both as contrast to the dedicated heroism of other characters, whose magnanimity is well proved by their having tolerated him, and as reflector of the war from a different perspective, Dagg is allowed to shift his fickle affections to a woman living safely further back in the mountains and to retire from the scene.

Of more concern to Johnston than Dagg or any of the other fictional characters was the war itself. Her development of the historical context in which the characters live and act has many of the virtues of her treatment of the war in *The Long Roll*. Her descriptions of the tactics which precede the battles and of the battles themselves convey a sense of accuracy and thoroughness few readers would find insufficient. A chapter describing the battle of Chickamauga in the Tennessee mountains—"one of the worst in history" (229)—is only one of several remarkably authentic recapturings of events. The report is not just straightforward narrative but also a composite of quoted eyewitness accounts, fictional dialogue of soldiers in the field, full reports of weather and atmospheric conditions, summaries of casualties (30,000), lists of major participants with brief biographical sketches ("Patrick Romayne Cleburne, —thirty-six years old, but with greying hair above his steel-grey eyes, Irishman of the county of Cork, one time soldier in the English army, then lawyer in the city of Helena and the State of Arkansas, then private in the Confederate army, then captain, then colonel, then brigadier, and now major-general . . .") (235), and identification of individual acts of heroism and tactics which decided the outcome. The account is obviously based on extensive research and reflects a desire to convey a realistic impression from all perspectives. Moreover, Johnston evidently wished to represent

all the various moods of war. On the one hand there is the sense of
pageantry, of war as a grand and glorious opportunity for men to
demonstrate courage and military prowess. The high point of this
mood, and of Confederate hopes and fortunes, is suggested in the
description of the review of troops ordered by General Lee in June
of 1863. The appearance of General Jeb Stuart epitomizes the
moment:

The sun strengthened, the mist began to lift, a number of bugles blared
together. Into the very atmosphere sifted something like golden laughter. A
shout arose—*Jeb Stuart!* . . .

Out of the misty forest, borne high, a vivid square in the sea of pearl,
came a large battle-flag. . . .

Stuart, followed by his staff, trotted from the forest. He wore his fighting
jacket and his hat with the plume, he was magnificiently mounted, he
stroked his wonderful, sunny beard, and he laughed with his wonderful,
sunny, blue eyes. He had more *verve* than any leader in that army. . . The
glory of the great fight hung about him like a golden haze, a haze that
magnified. . . (82-83)

Less than a year later, "They buried Jeb Stuart in Hollywood,
buried him with no pageantry of martial or of civil woe" (312).

As the mood of the war shifts to despair, it also reflects feelings of
fear and horror; both are amply established throughout the book in
detailed descriptions of bloodshed and violent death. Especially
effective in showing the horror of close combat is Johnston's
description of fighting at the "Bloody Angle":

The trenches grew slippery with blood. It mixed with the rain and ran in
red streamlets. The bayonet point felt first the folds of cloth, then it touched
and broke the skin, then it parted the tissues, then it grated against bone,
or, passing on, rending muscle and gristle, protruded, a crimson point. (303)

Troops on both sides are overwhelmed by the devastation effected
by the explosion of mines at Petersburg, which leave a crater thirty
feet deep; Johnston describes in detail the human consequences of
men blown apart or buried alive. As one reviewer commented, she
proved the Civil War "one of the cruelest and ghastliest happenings
of modern history."[32]

Her treatment of the nature and effects of war in *Cease Firing* conveys as successfully as *The Long Roll* the emotional impact as well as the facts. However, in two major ways her treatment of the historical context suffers by comparison with *The Long Roll.*

The first objection is that *Cease Firing* lacks the unifying focus of a central historical figure. The portraits of Lee and Johnston lack the quantity and kind of development which made that of Jackson dominate *The Long Roll.* Obviously the decision to collapse two projected novels into one restricted the space available for development of either figure, and the desire to give attention to both had the effect of making them compete for attention. As a result, neither portrait provides a cohesive element to bind together a large cast of characters spread over several geographical settings. The rapid shifts of scene and frequent introduction of new characters in *The Long Roll* never seemed as diffuse as in *Cease Firing* because all, including the fictional characters and the course of the war, were tied to Jackson; the attempt to convey more space and more widely scattered events created a greater need for such a figure in *Cease Firing,* but that need is not fulfilled.

The kind of development given Lee and Johnston is symptomatic of a more serious shortcoming. The stress throughout is upon the persistence and sagacity of the two figures, upon the qualities which lead to worship of heroes rather than respect for men. Lacking the raw material of Jackson's eccentricities to work with, Johnston might be expected to have had difficulty making the two seem as human; however, there is little evidence she had any intention to provide a balanced portrait. Instead, the evidence indicates that she allowed her personal and partisan interests to replace the objectivity for which she had struggled in *The Long Roll.*

Evidence of very personal interest is to be found in allusions to the war experiences of her father and descriptions of the effects of war upon her home community. The reader is informed of the placement of Major John William Johnston's battalion of artillery in Georgia and of the wounding of the commander—"twenty-five years old, brown-eyed, warm-hearted, sincere, magnetic, loved by his men" (273). The slave Tullius describes the burning of Buchanan and "a house by the mouth of the bridge" (349), undoubtedly a reference to her father's family home. While such allusions are neither obtrusive nor irrelevant, they demonstrate a personal concern which raises questions about the author's objectivity. Clearer evidence of partisan bias is to be found in comparisons of the behavior of Southern and Northern troops. A meaningful contrast was no doubt intended in descriptions of the caution with which Confederate troops treated private property and citizens during the invasion of Pennsylvania and the contrasting campaign of burning and looting conducted by Northern troops in Virginia and Georgia. Particularly criticized are Sheridan, who "devastated as thoroughly as if his name had been Attila" (382), and Sherman, who created a "swathe of misery, horror, and destruction" (406).

The clinching evidence of both personal and partisan bias lies in Johnston's comparisons of the roles of various Southern officers. The context of her comments may require some explanation. The aftermath of the war saw recriminations directed not just at the North but at what were interpreted as the errors and weaknesses of Southern military and political leaders by those who wished to place blame for the defeat. The result was a small library of works attacking or justifying the behavior and tactics of specific individuals. Johnston's cousin, General Joseph Eggleston Johnston, who had the misfortune to be in command during two major defeats and thus was already subject to criticism, added to the controversy by publishing in 1874 his *Narrative of Military Operations* in which he defended his own actions and freely criticized others, especially Jefferson Davis. One writer has said that, after Davis's reputation began to be rehabilitated, Johnston's book "was regarded with lofty suspicion and pointed to as an example of the bad taste which characterized so many former Confederates in the period of 'the Battle of the Books.' "[33]

Johnston wished to reply to critics of her cousin and set the record straight by marshaling evidence to prove that he had been given impossible tasks and had been deprived of the means to carry them out. Asked to delay Sherman, he did so but did not have the men or materials to conduct an offensive campaign. As testimony to the wisdom of his strategy she quotes directly from such opponents as "Fighting Joe Hooker" and Sherman, to whom she attributes the comment that " 'the Confederate Government rendered us most valuable service. Being dissatisfied with the Fabian policy of General Johnston, it relieved him and General Hood was substituted. . . . The character of a leader is a large factor in the game of war, and I confess I was pleased at this change' " (257).

Johnston's method may very well reflect an accurate appraisal of General Johnston's role, but it obviously is intensely partisan. Moreover, it fails to convey any real sense of the man. Had she provided the personal, humanizing detail necessary for a balanced portrait, she might have succeeded in overcoming the lack of both unity and objectivity which make *Cease Firing* less successful than *The Long Roll.*

The effect of her special pleading is consistent with the general atmosphere of the book. Such vivid scenes of the flooding of the Mississippi River and the appearance of the sun at Gettysburg seem calculated to evoke emotion, and there is much more lingering over the melancholy aspects of the lost cause than in *The Long Roll.* Adding these elements to the love story of Edward and Desiree reinforces the impression that *Cease Firing* is more conventional than *The Long Roll* both as fiction and as treatment of the war.

Most reviews were complimentary, generally equating *Cease Firing* with its companion volume. The opinion that "the two are our greatest stories of war"[34] was widely shared, and in more recent years Robert Lively has cited both as examples of the "true *historical novel.*"[35] Lively's further opinion that working in the genre was harmful to Johnston's career shows recognition of important changes, but the real causes of her later failures lie elsewhere.

CHAPTER 4

Causes

IF *LEWIS RAND* and the Civil War novels were written out of Mary Johnston's sense of duty to her family and region, that obligation was fulfilled at the same time she was developing other loyalties that seem almost contradictory. Foremost among these was a commitment to the cause of woman's suffrage. On 15 November 1909, she publicly denied any formal ties with " 'militant' " partisans of the woman's suffrage movement, stating that her interest was "neither more nor less" than in "stamping out tuberculosis . . . conserving our forests and . . . taking a little thought for the welfare of the generations who come after us."[1] But by the next month she had joined the movement and soon became an active public supporter. Her suffrage activities included attendance at conventions, the organization of local leagues, and, most significantly, articles and speeches.

At the same time she demonstrated a concern about other public issues. Calling herself a "sociologist," in February 1910 she publicly deplored the possibility that two Virginia universities would become "mercenaries of the predatory rich" by accepting gifts from the Carnegie Foundation.[2] She declined during the same year an invitation to write an article on socialism but said she was much in sympathy with "three great world movements": woman's suffrage, collective ownership of property, and the "freeing of religion from dogma."[3]

As soon as she had completed *Cease Firing*, she began a series of four works in which she became an advocate for those three causes. Despite great differences in subject and setting, the four have in common a challenge to traditional values and ways of life. They argue that such values may inhibit human development and freedom. They provided much controversy but little popular enthusiasm; Johnston, however, evidently was willing to endanger her career because of the intensity of her commitment.

Unfortunately, the works also have in common a decline in quality as fiction, for Johnston was no more successful than many of her peers in combining the roles of advocate and novelist. Still, despite their faults, the works are very significant as documents recording interests of the day, and they contain merits beyond those of propaganda.

I   Hagar (1913)

Hagar focuses upon the problem of society's treatment of women. It is the story of the gradually developing emancipation of one woman, Hagar Ashendyne, who learns she must struggle against both the specific legal restrictions placed upon women by society and the more subtle pressures of received opinion. The struggle focuses upon the specific cause of woman's suffrage but ranges beyond that issue as Hagar seeks self-fulfillment as a writer and personal integrity as an independent human being. In Johnston's concept of the nature of the struggle and the factors necessary to make it successful lie both the strengths and weaknesses of the novel. *Hagar* has serious shortcomings as fiction and as propaganda, but it shows a more perceptive awareness of the issues than was noted by most readers who praised or condemned it.

The early portion of *Hagar* displays the influences which ordinarily would produce a genteel, submissive Southern lady if the raw material, the young girl Hagar, were not exceptionally independent. Foremost among these influences are her grandparents, Colonel Argall Ashendyne and Old Miss, who rear her at their plantation, Gilead Balm, because their son has deserted Hagar and her mother. The mother resents but is too weak to rebel against the role assigned her, as epitomized by Old Miss:

"the Lord, for his own good purposes,—and it is *sinful* to question his purposes,—regulated society as it is regulated, and placed women where they are placed. No one claims—certainly I don't claim—that women as women do not see a great deal of hardship. The Bible gives us to understand that it is their punishment. Then I say take your punishment with meekness. It is possible that by doing so you may help earn remission for all."[4]

Early indications that Hagar may not submit meekly are shown in her troublesome questions about why women do not have money, her kindness to a young escaped convict, and her interest in reading dangerous books. Discovered reading Darwin's *Descent of Man*, she must seek forgiveness from the bishop and be denied books for a week.

The influences continue a few years later when Hagar, at age eighteen, is sent to a school conducted by Mrs. LeGrand, who has a "gift generally for preserving dew and bloom and ignorance of evil in her interesting charges" (29). Hagar's stay is cut short when an infatuation with one of the teachers offers her a chance to display independence, at the risk of falling into another kind of trap.

Some positive influences emerge at this stage of her development; she meets a few women who support themselves and have a larger vision of women's potential role in life. After winning a $200 prize for a short story, Hagar resolves to try to support herself by writing, and the pattern for her eventual escape is set. Her consciousness of the need to become independent and to do something important with her life, and her knowledge of the means to do both, are developed by a series of experiences in New York; she walks in the slums, attends Socialist meetings, talks with women who are oppressed and women who have found a purpose in life, renews her acquaintance with an escaped convict (now a speaker for Socialist causes), and continues to write stories with "metaphysical value" (249). An interlude of ten years spent traveling with her wealthy father, the last two caring for him after a stroke, brings maturity and a greater clarity of purpose; she decides to work actively for woman's suffrage while recognizing that the cause is only part of a larger struggle for human emancipation and growth. Rejecting for the third time the marriage offer of Ralph Coltsworth, her family's choice, she at last finds the kind of husband she can accept, a "comrade" (365), when she meets the bridge-builder John Fay. They confess their love while facing death during a storm at sea and, after being rescued, presumably will marry and live happily.

This happy conclusion does not carry with it much sense of conviction, and it is symptomatic of major faults in the novel, the unsatisfactory development of both plot and characters. The too conveniently available lover is only one example of artificially contrived incidents and implausible coincidences throughout the plot. One finds it unlikely that Hagar would by accident encounter the escaped convict Denny Gayde at a Socialist meeting in New York and utterly incredible that she would meet him again at a library in the Bahamas. Johnston does not manage well the task of bringing her elaborate cast of characters together under believable circumstances. Part of the problem is that the cast is too large; her desire to trace all of the complications and stages of Hagar's development over a period of about thirty years leads her to introduce too many characters and to make too many compromises; the plot becomes episodic, disjointed, and sketchy. Too many of the characters are mere abstractions, interchangeable names without faces, and the best developed characters, Colonel Ashendyne and Old Miss, succeed mainly as stereotypes reflecting the traditional values Hagar must reject. Hagar's father, Medway, is particularized as a lovable Hedonist whose selfishness is most dangerous because of his attractive qualities, but he enters and disappears from the novel almost as an afterthought, long after Hagar is in real danger of being diverted from her goals. It is obvious that Johnston was preoccupied almost exclusively with the development of Hagar; all the other characters are mere foils.

And even in the case of Hagar, Johnston's success is mixed. The portrait of Hagar is most complete early in the novel, when the issue of her escape from the submissive role expected of women is still in doubt. The conflicts she faces as a child and young girl are adequately developed, and the quantity and quality of detail provided to establish her character are convincing. Johnston is especially cautious to show that the young Hagar has no extraordinary human qualities that would allow her to triumph over insurmountable odds. The brief romance with the teacher, Edgar Laydon, is a good example of the skill with which Johnston handles this stage of Hagar's development; Hagar is shown to be susceptible to romantic yearnings, and she is saved from a bad marriage mainly because her honesty leads her to report her plans to her grandfather, who breaks off the match.

It is in the second half of the book, after Hagar's escape seems assured, that the portrait is less convincing. The main conflict of her later years concerns what specific course she will follow to fulfill herself, and Johnston does not succeed in making that an interesting human problem because she renders it undramatically. She is obviously more interested in the causes and ideas to which Hagar is exposed than in the character herself, and the character becomes both abstract and unbelievable. Hagar attains a level of self-assurance, tolerance, and independence which represents a worthy, but not very believable, ideal.

These flaws in plot and character development were apparent to most early readers. Many reviewers perceived *Hagar* as a pivotal novel in Mary Johnston's career and feared that it represented a turn for the worse. The novel's topicality brought it widespread attention—Johnston's clipping service sent well over 300 reviews—but only modest praise. The pattern of response is, as one might expect, much related to the reviewers' degree of sympathy with the woman's suffrage movement, but even some who were sympathetic to the cause thought *Hagar* unsuccessful as fiction. While several reviewers were impressed by the early portion, most objected to the second half because it too much resembled a tract. Representative of the reviews is that by Helen Bullis in the *New York Times:* she found the young Hagar "as real as David Copperfield" but objected to the direct exposition, rather than dramatization, of the suffragist position.[5] The consensus was that *Hagar* failed because it sacrificed adequate development of the plot and characters to the interests of arguing for the cause.

This explanation is only partly true. One has only to consider the episodic plots and stereotyped characters of Johnston's earlier works to find another possible explanation for the faults of *Hagar*. In her earlier novels she constructed plots on the grand scale and often seemed to be striving deliberately to make use of character types; such methods are both expected and excusable in a novel which does not pretend to be more than a Romance of Adventure. It is very possible that the faults of *Hagar* are less the result of a change in approach to fiction or a decline of talent than of an attempt to incorporate customary methods into a work where they are less appropriate. Certainly some such process has taken place in the use of nature as a backdrop for much of the action of the novel. While in earlier works Johnston skillfully made use of settings as integral parts of the novels, her similar but perfunctory attempts to use nature to convey Hagar's mystical identity with the large forces at work in the universe do not succeed.

In focusing upon the novel's shortcomings, most commentators have either misunderstood or neglected a significant accomplishment in *Hagar*. Johnston's analysis of the problems of women is much more complex than was apparent to many readers. In what is otherwise a perceptive review, Helen Bullis argued that Johnston "confuses the ills which women suffer because they are women with the ills which they suffer because they are not voters" and fails to recognize that "most human ills are remediable only by the slow processes of evolution."[6] The judgment is astonishing, for those points are the heart of Johnston's analysis. She demonstrates perceptively and in detail that getting the right to vote is only a necessary precondition toward reforming a lengthy list of abuses, many of which are tied directly to larger problems that affect men as well as women. She shows, in fact, that many of the problems women face are the result of archaic laws and customs which restrict women's rights to hold property and earn money; many of Hagar's conflicts are traceable to her desire to be financially independent. Johnston also shows that a marriage relationship in which one party treats the other as property can be damaging to both. Hagar's friend Rachel Bolt's Marriage is a " 'sink and a pit and a horror' " (217) because her husband has abused her sexually and had relations with other women, leading to venereal disease and ultimately to blindness in their second child. These problems are shown to be connected to the larger public issues of poverty, urban blight, and mistreatment of labor which concern Hagar's socialist friends, and all of the problems are shown ultimately to be the result of a need for greater tolerance and respect for the rights and dignity of all human beings. *Hagar* is an argument for a broader emancipation of the human spirit than was reflected in most persons' concept of woman's suffrage.

Furthermore, Johnston shows that the reform of society is indeed a slow process of evolution, to be accomplished only when man has evolved into something other than the weak, ignorant, selfish creature called human. Hagar has no hopes to reform the " 'featherless biped' " (308) Ralph Coltsworth, a pitiable atavistic survival, but instead hopes that a better form of human being will evolve. In a key passage of the novel she describes the expected process to Denny Gayde; after characterizing the evolution of life through various stages from "Amphibian" through "our brother the chimpanzee" (293) to the point it became human, she says, " 'Like that ancestral tribe, we are growing, we are changing—we feel a strange new life within us . . . we need a new word' " (294). She answers affirmatively Denny's question whether " 'the movement of women toward freedom of field and toward self-recognition—no less than the general movement toward socialization—is part of the change' " (294).

This viewpoint is connected directly to some threads of development in Johnston's thought which were lost upon readers who dismissed *Hagar* as feminist propaganda. Of special interest to the student of her career is a dinner party scene where are gathered a Fabian Socialist, a scientist who is interested in psychical research, a suffragist, and a woman essayist who has written about eugenics, all "incurably hopeful, though at quite long range, as reformers have to be" (250). Their community of interests is very much a reflection of Johnston's own concern and hopes: they clearly anticipate topics that would dominate later works.

Also of special interest to the student of Johnston's career is the difficult problem of the extent to which the novel is autobiographical. Those familiar with her suffrage activities naturally assumed, as did the reviewer in *The Woman Voter*, that it was "open to more than a suspicion of autobiography,"[7] and some of the specific problems identified, most notably the economic ones, are the same problems Johnston faced in her personal life. Ample evidence is available to suggest that Hagar's struggle to overcome a " 'Brahmin-like attitude' " (286), to in Denny's words " 'be in one brain Socialist and Individualist' "(287), was Johnston's problem, too; she became a suffrage worker quite reluctantly. Moreover, some of the details of Hagar's life, especially in the early portion of the novel, are based at least loosely upon Johnston's childhood experiences. Some, such as descriptions of conversations overheard by a young girl on board a packet boat, seem to have been taken directly from Johnston's diaries. Remembering that she also read Darwin, attended a girl's school, and wished to become a writer, one is tempted to conclude that the novel is more autobiographical than has been recognized.

However, not all available evidence points toward an autobiographical reading. The harsh judgment of Hagar's family does not accord at all with the attitudes Johnston expresses toward her own family everywhere else, and, as noted earlier, the portraits seem to be type characters; it seems unlikely that they convey an accurate impression of Johnston's attitude toward her own childhood. The pattern of Hagar's later years does not correspond except in quite general ways to Johnston's experiences. In light of the contradictory evidence, one must agree with Lawrence Nelson, who doubts that it is autobiography but says it "comes closest perhaps to telling the truth of the inner life of Virginia's foremost historical novelist."[8] *Hagar* is an imaginative projection of some of Johnston's ideals rather than a faithful recording of her own self-estimate.

It is a puzzling and disappointing work, but its faults help one understand the latter half of Johnston's writing career. For several years she attempted to use her novels as a vehicle for various causes and ideas, and she was never entirely successful in doing so.

II   The Witch *(1914)*

Mary Johnston's next novel shows a continuing concern with the issues of the evolving human spirit, the status of women, the possibilities of a new human consciousness, and the need for freedom of thought. Evidently her concern about the reception accorded *Hagar*, however, led her to abandon plans for another novel set in the present and dealing directly with the feminist cause, and to write instead a novel intended to be historical romance. *The Witch* is set in the early seventeenth century, primarily in England, and portrays two main characters whose lives are intertwined through shared persecution and love. Gilbert Aderhold, a physician, scientist, and skeptic, and Joan Heron, accused of witchcraft, are pursued as heretics. Though the historical context made the novel more palatable to her contemporaries, Johnston's criticism of the ignorance and intolerance which make outcasts of the two obviously is addressed also to attitudes which survived into her own time.

The early chapters depict the developing intensity of religious controversy in the years following the death of Elizabeth I; men mistrust each other and fear the church and the devil. Aderhold, a fugitive correctly suspected of apostasy, becomes a physician in the remote village of Hawthorn and resolves to keep his opinions to himself. The viewpoint shifts to Joan, who is too beautiful and cheerful to escape envy and suspicion, and who narrowly escapes the lust of Harry Carthew, a Puritan jealous of her brief meetings with Aderhold. Meanwhile, Aderhold has been rumored to be a sorcerer and alchemist and is warned to leave when his past is accidentally discovered. He refuses to go, because he is needed to treat victims of the plague. The Puritan zealot Master Thomas Clement, minister at Hawthorn, insures that both are accused, convicted, and imprisoned, but they escape in disguise as Giles and John Allen and embark for Virginia. When Joan's identity accidentally is discovered, they are set adrift in a small boat. Rescued by Indians, the two live happily with them on an island until a Spanish boat arrives and lays waste to the village, killing their infant daughter, Hope. Escaping the Spanish, Aderhold and Joan are found by an English ship and cannot avoid returning to England after an absence of six years. By chance encountering Clement and Carthew, they are denounced as sorcerer and witch; their love and the philosophy they have developed sustain them as they reenter prison and wait to be hanged.

Johnston's idea for the novel, outlined in a "Note for Heretic and Witch (or some such title)," reveals what she thought it must accomplish:

The whole a romance but with a meaning below the romance. More psychological work than my earlier stories, but adventure and acting and drama enough I think. The man really is a heretic, the woman likewise. The sympathies of the reader are supposed to go with both.

Clearly she hoped that *The Witch* would recapture her audience, that it would at the same time be a serious and realistic novel probing depths of character and considering issues of great consequence, and that it would allow her to make a specific plea for freedom of thought.

The Witch was a modest success when measured against both her intentions and more objective criteria. The major weaknesses in the book may be traced to the fact that the intentions were contradictory enough to require some compromises which are not successful. Some of the conventions of the Romance of Adventure are evident in various aspects of *The Witch*, but they are combined with other effects which make them seem inappropriate. The plot, for example, indeed contains "adventure and acting and drama enough"—to the detriment of other elements. As in so many of her novels, Johnston tried to cover too much time and space. The sequence of the whole six years of Aderhold and Joan's absence from England provides excitement enough, but it seems to interrupt a chain of events which moves inevitably toward the conclusion. One reviewer may have exaggerated in saying that the novel "degenerates into sheer melodrama" after having been a "consistent, firmly knit story,"[9] but what excitement Johnston gained was achieved at the expense of what could have been a well-unified plot. The whole escape sequence seems melodramatic when measured against the dramatic intensity of the trial scene before the Witch Judge.

Similarly, the characters reflect some inconsistency of purpose. Aderhold and Joan face conflicts which would seem to make them anything but candidates for a conventionally romantic love story, and Johnston wavered in dealing with the problem; their love never becomes the dominant concern and seems instead an unnecessary concession to the requirements of romance. The fact that their love is more comradeship than passion probably is an echo of the feminist argument developed extensively in *Hagar*. A more serious problem is that Johnston was so intent upon making them sympathetic that she did not make them human. Their heresy is shown to be at the same time a state of prelapsarian innocence and an anticipation of an evolutionary form of human striving for perfection; they learn to be tolerant and forgiving of their accusers because they have the power to see a future when men can become more than men. Only the rigidly orthodox could find fault with the broad principles of their beliefs, but Johnston was much more successful in evoking real sympathy for the two when she displayed their human conflicts.

Much more interesting and much more purposefully developed are the characters Carthew and Clement. To be sure, Carthew has many of the qualities of a conventional villain; he tries to rape Joan and later remains silent when his confession might save her from being convicted as a witch. However, the analysis of his motives and his rationalizations involves a depth of insight not ordinarily accorded such a character type. He tries to persuade Joan to love him rather than Aderhold because he is " 'one who sinneth truly and puts oftentimes in peril his immortal soul, but is at least no misbeliever and denier of God's Word.' "[10] The specific nature of his illogical hypocrisy marks him as partaking of the attitudes Johnston wishes to attack, but he is much simpler and less dangerous in her view than Master Clement, whose zeal for ferreting out doubters is actually a psychological compensation for the doubts he refuses to admit to himself. She shows that he sees Aderhold's greatest sin in his refusal to admit that he is a sinner; Clement cannot tolerate an attitude which challenges the authority of his belief. Johnston's portrait of Clement is skillfully drawn without benefit of the conventions of romance, and it is central to her argument.

The atmosphere of the novel also is skillfully established. *The Witch* has, considering the melodramatic quality of some of the episodes, a remarkably consistent tone throughout, an atmosphere of gloom and impending disaster which is in part a reflection of the time and place and in part a foreboding expectancy about the fate of the main characters. One suspects that in establishing the tone, as well as the setting (including even the name of the village), Johnston used as model the romances of Hawthorne rather than the Romance of Adventure. The mood of the time is conveyed by authentic details; Johnston was well versed about the customary procedures for dealing with heretics and witches and about the state of mind which made such procedures necessary. Aderhold's difficulty in even drinking a cup of ale without harassment about his religious sympathies shows the hysteria and violence of the period. His encounters with various bigots and victims of superstition both establish a sense of the time and place and provide warning of the danger to come.

The sense of foreboding is overdone in one respect only. While Aderhold and Joan have little past experience to suggest that their happiness on the island will last, their sudden premonition of disaster just before the Spanish attack does strain credibility. Johnston had previously attributed to Aderhold a power of "sudden interfusion, or permeation, or intensity of realization" (63), much like the kind she had experienced herself and was soon to write about frequently. But, though crediting Aderhold with psychic powers may be consistent characterization, it is more convincing in *The Witch* than in later works. The action of the novel offered sufficient foreshadowing of events to come without this device.

While reviewers, of course, did not have the advantage of hindsight which would allow them to respond fully to Johnston's developing interest in mysticism, one reviewer did think it her most mature and best novel because it was concerned "with more vital things, things essentially of the spirit."[11] Most responses were directed toward her treatment of the issues, for which she was praised, and toward the extent to which the novel matched her earlier work, about which there was disagreement. One reviewer said she had returned to "her earlier and more attractive manner,"[12] while another thought *The Witch* was, like her other recent novels, "too gruesome to be quite healthy."[13] Most hostile was the reviewer who said:

Such material as this presented in a pseudo-historical novel is as incongruous as would be John the Baptist preaching in a ruffed velvet and a sword. One might dismiss it as unimportant if Miss Johnston's other work had not prepared us for something excellent of its kind, something that not only read like *Sir Mortimer* but attained the same attractiveness of subject and unity of style.[14]

The response certainly demonstrates that Johnston had not succeeded in recapturing a portion of her audience interested primarily in the Romance of Adventure.

Considering that Johnston was engaged at the time in suffrage work, in the construction of Three Hills, and in trying to meet the conflicting demands of her public and her own voice, the modest successes of *The Witch* are more remarkable than its shortcomings. Its greatest weakness is also its greatest strength; though to Johnston's audience less obviously a tract than *Hagar*, *The Witch* is primarily important in her career as her most bitter attack upon intolerance.

III   The Fortunes of Garin (1915)

Turning farther back in time to eleventh century France as setting for her next novel, Johnston seemed intent upon satisfying her publishers and that portion of her audience disappointed that her recent novels had lacked the high-spirited and colorful excitement of her earlier work. *The Fortunes of Garin* is a story of love and adventure, complete with a chivalrous knight, a maiden to be protected and won, and a villainous feudal lord to be overcome. Johnston's introduction of social issues as an element of the conflict and her portrait of a quite unconventional heroine, however, both show that she had not lost interest in the causes which had dominated her recent work and rescue the book from some excesses of the Romance of Adventure.

The story opens with the young esquire Garin debating whether to remain in service to his not so prosperous lord, Raimbaut the Six-Fingered, or to take advantage of an opportunity to go into the church. Both choices are lost and he must flee, however, after he interrupts the intended rape of a herd-girl, Jael, by the powerful knight, Jaufre of Montmaure, who is feared by lords and church alike. After falling in love with a veiled lady he sees in a grove of laurels, Garin becomes a troubadour and knight, pursuing his "Unattainable Ideal."[15] He goes on a crusade to Syria and, seven years later, has established a reputation as Garin de l'Isle d'Or, who pursues a love described in song as his "Fair Goal."

Garin returns home to help defend Roche-de-Frêne when he learns that the lord of Montmaure has ravaged the countryside and laid seige to the castle because Gaucelm the Fortunate would not marry his daughter, Audiart, called the "Ugly Princess," to Jaufre. Despite the support given Gaucelm by the developing middle class in return for favors granted, Jaufre seems poised to triumph because he has the support of Duke Richard. However, Audiart continues the struggle after Gaucelm's death and develops a scheme to get Richard's support; she and Garin go in disguise, and she persuades

Richard Lion Heart to withdraw his troops, breaking the siege.
Along the way Garin learns that Audiart was both Jael and his Fair
Goal, and she invites him to propose.

This thin and predictable plot, the idealized characters whose
story it develops, and most particularly the focus upon details of
dress and manners of the medieval setting are the elements which
make *The Fortunes of Garin* resemble the Romance of Adventure.
The plot offers some opportunities for vivid scenes and exciting
conflict, the most dramatic among them the battle scene in which
Audiart leads a troop of knights and loyal burghers to save the day.
Garin and his jongleur friend Elias of Montaudon seem calculated
to match the conventional stereotype of characters in medieval
romance; they consciously seek a love to serve, and they spend
much of their time composing songs and going on quests. Johnston's
use of the terminology of horsemanship and armory and her
elaborate descriptions of costume assume an audience which both
expected and was knowledgeable about details of the medieval
setting, no doubt from the experience of reading many similar
novels.

Evidently she succeeded in fulfilling the expectations of most
readers; the reviews were predominantly favorable, calling it, for
example, "lively romance."[16] Evidently also the expectations were
not very demanding, because Johnston certainly did not avail herself
of·all the opportunities offered by the subject matter. Some key
incidents are treated rather briefly, and much of the action is
rendered in expository rather than dramatic form. Even reviewers
who liked the book were disappointed that she was "a little too
meditative . . . more like an essayist"[17] and failed to dramatize the
interview between Richard and Audiart.[18]

Many of the characters are not well developed, even as stereotypes; Johnston relied on tag lines to particularize most of them.
Even the setting is occasionally slighted; Gaucelm's castle is described in only enough detail to give a very general impression. Her
use of phrases such as "this or that sweet strain" (146) and "fair-to-
middling voice" (13) to describe singing do not indicate much
interest in precision. One must conclude either that Johnston
assumed the reader already knew the story, the characters, and the
setting well enough to supply the omitted details or that her own
interest lay elsewhere.

One suspects her underlying purpose was to display her interpretation of the causes for the disintegration of the feudal system and

to show the elements of change which she had identified as signs of evolutionary progress toward a better social order. She wished to show that the barbarism of the age and the opportunism of the church were to be challenged by a rising middle class, by a new ideal of love, by a more rational concept of justice toward all mankind, including women, and by the development of new powers of heightened human consciousness. These forces are, of course, a direct reflection of the causes in which she was interested and of her developing interest in a mystical philosophy, and they explain some elements of the novel which seem not to fit the genre of costume romance.

One such element is the surprising amount of attention given to details about the growth of trade and the granting of privileges to those once "wholly servile" (74). The material is made integral to the action of the novel when Gaucelm's progressive attitude toward the townspeople brings their support against the lords of Mont-maure, who still rule absolutely, but the material is not included just as a device to give probability to the plot. Nor are the portraits of churchmen interested mainly in preserving their political power included only to establish the conflicts within the novel: Johnston wished to show that the church's power to produce a gloomy atmosphere of religious fervor, even if persisting into her own time, is doomed.

Even more surprising in a novel ostensibly a romance are aspects of the portrait of Audiart. She is called the Ugly Princess because her virtues include intelligence rather than beauty; she lacks the gifts of conventional charm most prized in an age of chivalric love. More importantly, she is far ahead of her time in questioning her status as a woman. She is independent and wishes no favors because of her sex; she wishes to play chess "fairly," not "courtly" (144). She even questions the whole code of chivalry when, rescued as Jael from Jaufre, she tells Garin,

"I am not very weak. Is it man's part, too, to lay hands upon a woman against her will? If man did not that, then man need not do, at such cost, the other. What credit to put water on the house you yourself set afire?" (27)

Her willingness and ability to defend her people during the siege are qualities which round out a portrait of the feminist ideal Johnston admired. Audiart is an anachronism in the contexts of both history and the Romance of Adventure, but she lends interest to the novel in ways that compensate for any inconsistency.

Beside her portrait, that of Garin is a disappointment. Completely dominated by the chivalric ideal, he chooses knighthood in spite of the knowledge that it is not all glamour. He is true to the chivalric ideal in worrying about being unfaithful to his Fair Goal when he falls in love with Audiart, but such consistency does little to make him a credible character. His most curious feature is his capacity to experience on several occasions "a deep and harmonious vibration, an expansion and intensification of being" (68). As motive for his behavior it is not very convincing, but it illustrates the kind of motivation Johnston came increasingly to use. It is a sign of her movement away from current issues and toward commitment to the mystical philosophy which further alienated her audience.

The Fortunes of Garin is not one of Johnston's best novels, but, if war in Europe had not adversely affected sales, it had at least the potential to help restore her popularity. Several years would pass before that could be said about another of her works.

IV   The Wanderers *(1917)*

The Wanderers is a sequence of nineteen short stories with different sets of principal characters and different settings in time and place, but it is so unified by significant aspects of content and form that it also must be evaluated as a novel. The stories develop themes central to Johnston's concerns, especially the status of women and the evolution of society, and the work as a whole shows stages of progress on both fronts. The principal characters in each story are eventually revealed as the same characters reincarnated; *The Wanderers* thus shows a unity of design but also anticipates a decline in Johnston's interest in the causes of her own time in favor of what she thought was a broader view of human affairs.

The sequence begins in primitive times and moves forward to the end of the eighteenth century. The earliest stories show problems of survival against hunger and wild animals before the development of a social order. In "The Forest," woman discovers the power of a stick as weapon against beasts, but man uses it to knock her down. In "The Cave" and "Big Trouble," women are shown to be the "authoritative sex"[19] because they are the organizers of society; men are "powerful encroachers" (32) because of their strength and, by the fourth story, "Property," have become dominant. After three stories which show further losses of status and power, "The Priestess of Marduk," set in ancient Babylon, shows woman reduced to the role of prostitute, a situation explored in greater detail in "Glaucon and Myrina." The Athenian Glaucon tells his wife to be content with her home and children while he seeks entertainment with the courtesan Myrina, because the gods have made two separate ways for men and women. However, he also wants Myrina to show him the same loyalty as would a wife. "The Pearl of the Deep" deals with the intrigue of seraglio politics and ends in a blood bath of revenge. After this story the gradual reconciliation of the sexes begins: it is developed in "The Banks of Jumuna" and "Valerian and Valeria." The path is not smooth, however, because the church stands as a barrier; five of the last seven stories show the adverse effects of Christianity upon the relations between the sexes. In "Alleda and Alaran," Alleda has to offer herself as a virgin sacrifice to convert a tribe of Goths. Dorotheus and Dorothea of "The Hermits" are ascetics who live in the desert and abandon their friendship when sinful passion is aroused. In "The End of the World," Gersonde is burned as a witch because she confounds the church by denying that the apocalypse will accompany the approaching millennium. The principals of "Thekla and Eberhard" hope that a new religious movement will bring greater freedom for women but discover that Martin Luther "preached the subjection of women" (387). The sixteenth story, "Moonlight," and the last story, "Jean and Espérance," develop Johnston's idea of the means for reconciliation. In the former, Beatrix and Tanneguy have a relation that transcends the physical, and they trace their history together from days in the forest and cave. Jean and Espérance, revolutionaries espousing the "Freedom of Woman" (415) in Paris of 1791, are at peace with each other as they recall their conflicts in previous lives, and they face death as only a temporary interruption of their life together in the future.

Individual stories develop specific conflicts and issues impossible to summarize briefly here, but Johnston was interested primarily in the main conflicts already outlined here. Her interests and the plans she developed for both the content and form of *The Wanderers* are revealed in letters to Julia Tutwiler, who acted as literary agent in attempts to place some of the stories in magazines after Johnston despaired of getting the work published in serial form. Johnston recognized the collection was too "episodic" and lacking in suspense to succeed as a serial, but she hoped some chapters could be published separately because they were "meant to be a serious contribution toward the growing mass of literature dealing consciously with this or the other aspect of the relations between the sexes, and with evolutionary sociology generally." Her earnestness about the work, and her attitude toward all of the work of her middle and later years, is indicated by her comment that she had "gone out of the thriller business."[20]

Choosing to develop the issues in a closely related series of stories that also could be regarded as self-contained units was an interesting and ambitious scheme which created special problems for the writer and for the critic. Desiring to show at the same time that the stories are different and yet the same basic story, Johnston sensed a need to provide both static and dynamic elements. Her solutions to the special problems of plot, characterization, setting, and tone work well enough to deserve more credit than that given her by contemporary reviews.

The plots within stories are not uniformly developed, but the overall plot has a unity provided by features other than just similar themes and characters. It is a rather mechanical device, but Johnston's description of seven of the first nine female principals as having some shade of red hair foreshadows increasingly stronger hints that the characters are reincarnations. Some stories end with conflicts not resolved, but one can hardly object when one considers that the point of such stories as "The Forest" is to delineate the lines of developing conflict. An unresolved conflict of "Big Trouble," whether the deity is male or female, must be seen as foreshadowing the larger role played by religion in subjugating women in later stories. One is less satisfied with the ending of "Glaucon and Myrina" because the issue over which they quarrel seems avoided rather than settled. One also could object that the reconciliations of the later stories are not well explained but could not argue that they violate the pattern Johnston established. Readers familiar with her other works may conclude that the overall plot is less disjointed than those of some of her novels.

Space limitations did not allow for full character development within any one story, and setting constitutes the chief means of particularizing characters and distinguishing them from each other. They are defined as types representative of the age in which they live rather than as individuals. That can be seen as a fault, however, only by ignoring the larger context. Though one reviewer thought reincarnation is "never insisted upon and often disappears,"[21] one

must not forget that they *are* the same character. And one should
not forget that Johnston often resorted to stereotyping as a means of
characterization.

It also was impossible to develop adequately nineteen different
historical settings, and Johnston made only a few efforts to do so;
one was accuracy in the kind of language used by the characters,
which develops from noises unintelligible to modern man in "The
Forest" through more sophisticated language appropriate to each
time. Mainly, however, she consistently focuses attention upon the
natural setting as a continuing frame of reference, just as she had
frequently done in earlier works. While more details would be
needed to convey a real sense of time and place, enough are
included to serve her purpose of marking significant stages of and
influences upon the changing status of women and society.

The intended and actual tone of *The Wanderers* do not coincide
exactly, but the discrepancy is the result of an inconsistency
Johnston would not have recognized. She intended that the feelings
generated by the stories would reflect the pattern of the status of
women and society. The developing conflict between the sexes was
to reach its "nadir" in "The Pearl of the Deep," and then the
gradual reconciliation of the sexes would lead to an increasing note
of hope for the future. But the stories have an unrelieved seriousness
and thinly veiled outrage at the treatment of women thoughout,
and few readers are likely to understand, much less accept, the basis
for optimism. Johnston apparently sensed no inconsistency in arguing on the one hand that women face real conflicts that require an
alteration of society and on the other that progress is inevitable.
Most readers are likely to find her analysis of the problem more
convincing than the solution; the actual tone of the book is more
consistent than her intentions would have allowed.

The modest successes of the book justify more enthusiastic
responses than it received. Most reviewers thought *The Wanderers*
too ambitious. Its publication during wartime probably accounts for
decreased interest, but only some basic misunderstanding of her
purposes and accomplishments could have led to such overreactions
as dismissing it as a "grindstone for the feminist axe"[22] and calling
it a "mercilessly tense and tedious document."[23] One reviewer's
comment that it is "tinted (or tainted) with metempsychosis"[24] is
perceptive in recognizing what is the main flaw in the book. Having
once again argued the cause of freedom *from* religion as well as the
causes of freedom for women and reformation of society, Johnston

tried to cap her argument with an exposition of a philosophical position which is inappropriate in the context. Her interest in occult sciences had led her to discover Theosophy, and the emphasis upon reincarnation and a mystical sense of oneness led to a vagueness of style and an abandonment of conflict which were to plague later works and which reduce the effectiveness of what is otherwise an undeservedly neglected work.

CHAPTER 5

Mystical Idealism

A T THE same time she was writing the works devoted to causes, Johnston had begun to curtail her active involvement in suffrage work and to shift the focus of her attention to other matters. One change involved renewal of her interest in colonial history; she honored the request of Yale University Press to contribute a volume to the "Chronicles of America Series." *Pioneers of the Old South* (1918) is primarily a brief narrative account of events and persons among early settlers in the South, but it contains some dramatizations of episodes. Reviewers generally thought her approach appropriate and praised the accuracy of her account, though one critic thought devoting most of the book to Virginia a sign of imbalance.[1]

Johnston's main interest lay elsewhere, and the three works which followed display a withdrawal into mysticism. The change in her work was so substantial that critics such as Grant Overton mistakenly are led to divide her career into two phases.[2] But ample evidence is available in earlier works to demonstrate that Johnston's interest in mysticism had evolved over several years and several works.

Personal experiences undoubtedly were somewhat responsible for the change. It is difficult to determine whether travel in Europe and Africa, the building of Three Hills, and controversy over the reception of her works, which eventually led to a change of publishers, were causes or consequences of the transformation, but certainly Johnston's developing concern about her personal experiences of heightened consciousness and her interest in Theosophy were more than coincidental. The three works published between 1918 and 1920 reflect both recent and continuing interests but are primarily distinguishable as the first and, with the exception of *The Exile* (1927), the only ones of her works to be dominated by her mystical philosophy. They marked the low point of her popularity, and they remain today the most disappointing of her works. For a short period thereafter Johnston experimented with other literary forms before attempting to recapture her audience by returning to the kind of novel which had first brought her success.

I Foes *(1918)*

The effectiveness of *Foes* as fiction was substantially diluted because it was the first of Johnston's novels not just to espouse but to be dominated by her belief in a mystical, supernatural philosophy. It is especially disappointing because it contains much unrealized potential as fiction; it portrays a quest by Alexander Jardine, who seeks vengeance against his boyhood friend, Ian Rullock, for causing the suicide of Elspeth Barrow, whom Alexander loved. While the basic conflict is by no means original, it had considerable potential for melodramatic, if not tragic, development, The potential of the historical setting of Scotland during the Jacobite rebellion certainly had been demonstrated by Johnston's predecessors, notably Walter Scott, and the ties between the principal characters and the political and religious factions of the day offered a mixture with potentially compelling interest. However, the plot comes to a peculiar resolution, the characters are transformed without comprehensible explanation, and the setting becomes irrelevant as Johnston attempts to demonstrate the workings of a power of heightened consciousness to overcome conflict and particular historical circumstances.

Ominous portents of conflict, danger, secret designs, and dark motives are established early in the novel by reference not only to the political and religious controversies of Scotland in 1735 but also to the atmosphere of superstition. The young boys Alexander and Ian, meeting for the first time, sense they have met before and have feelings of both attraction and repulsion they cannot explain. Their friendship overcomes family differences and is supposedly sealed when Alexander rescues Ian from drowning in the Kelpie's Pond, a place inhabited by frightening spirits. Nine years later, however, Ian returns to court Elspeth, who has rejected Alexander's love; they fall in love instantly and passionately and with conviction they, too, have loved before. After Ian leaves to become involved in the Jacobite plot, Alexander finds the body of Elspeth floating in the Kelpie's Pond. Because pregnant and abandoned, she had become despondent. He has his first opportunity for vengeance during the battles of Prestonpans and Culloden, but he swoons after being wounded by Ian, who escapes. The scene shifts to Spain, where

Alexander ransoms Ian from robbers, to Paris, where a second fight is interrupted by seconds after Alexander is slightly wounded, and to Rome, where the two help each other escape from a cave-in of ancient passages; outside Rôme, on the Campagna, Alexander has a moment of higher consciousness which persuades him to give up seeking revenge. Three years later Alexander and Ian are fully reconciled, and Alexander accompanies Ian in escaping Scotland for India.

So successfully did Johnston establish the nature and degree of conflict between Alexander and Ian that their reconciliation seems to reflect improbable plotting and inconsistent characterization. From the outset Alexander is shown to be fated toward a life of seeking revenge; as a child, he is overcome by emotion upon hearing a story of vengeance, and his father's deathbed charge is to fight his enemy when he ·finds him. Discovering it is to be Ian, he gives himself wholly to the quest. Ian, too, is developed as a character fated for conflict; he readily adopts the role of rebel and conspirator, and his treatment of Elspeth is in part attributed to an inherent "drop of malice,"[3] a desire to hurt Alexander. Their successive meetings in some respects seem calculated to deepen the division between them; Alexander's wounds cause less physical suffering than injured pride, and his relentless pursuit makes Ian feel that he has become the offended party. The developing conflict seems to point toward a violent and tragic climax, and the sudden reversal might be interpreted as the sentimental, illogical, but perhaps expected happy ending of a Romance of Adventure.

Yet the transformation and reconciliation are neither inconsistent with Johnston's plan nor illogical in terms of the mystical philosophy she had adopted. Concurrent with the developing conflict she suggests forces at work which will unite the two. She attributes to both a sense that their fates are intertwined and to Alexander especially a series of moments of increased awareness, a "ghostly afterglow" (276), which surprise him because they contradict rather than reinforce his vengeful purposes. The sense that all boundaries of time and space are transcended in a spirit of unity which comes to him outside Rome is the culmination of the pattern Johnston wished to establish as more important than the conflict between the two— a pattern of discovery rather than confrontation.

Moreover, she wished to show that their fates are not only larger than they recognize but also part of a design for the universe. Not very subtle hints are dropped throughout that they are to be seen as reincarnations of foes in previous lives. One learns, for example, that Elspeth's beauty reminds one character of pictures seen in Italy and that Ian has " 'a dash . . . of what you might call the Borgia' " (117). The conflict is obviously to be seen as one stage in a continuing, evolving movement toward a future life in a world without conflict, a Theosophical paradise.

Evidently Johnston wished to develop the conflict and characters not for their dramatic possibilities but in order to highlight, by contrast, the supernatural forces which effect the reconciliation. Edward Wagenknecht argues that the message is not overt propaganda and that the reconciliation follows inevitably "once all the elements of the situation have been taken into account." However, he also notes that "the ordinary novelist"[4] would have ended the book tragically, an important concession when one measures the success of *Foes* as fiction, and it is difficult to agree with his high praise for the book as something other than fiction. The novel fails to make Johnston's belief vivid and convincing because the conflict and characters are too credible in human terms to be overshadowed by unseen and, for that matter, unshowable forces. It fails as fiction because her beliefs deny the significance of the characters' current lives and attempt to remove from the center of attention the element of conflict essential to fiction.

The problem is further revealed in her treatment of the setting. She provides ample evidence early in the book that the main characters are products of their environments; however, she wished to show at the same time that they must learn to transcend such artificial barriers as geography, time, and even their physical presence. Her belief might have led her to make the novel completely ahistorical. Fortunately, old habits assert themselves to the extent that she portrays the natural environment consistently well throughout, but particulars of time and place become increasingly less relevant as the book progresses.

Attempts by writers such as Wagenknecht to find merit in it are somewhat strained. *Foes* is disappointing because of the opportunities missed. Had Johnston made better use of the conflict, the historical setting, and her interest in her Scottish forebears, the book might have been excellent historical fiction. Had she stressed the latent pacifism, it might at least have matched the success of others devoted to causes of this world. But the commitment to mysticism evidently required that she abandon for a while the qualities which had made her previous work interesting. In doing so, she established a pattern, best described by an anonymous critic, which carried through the next two works: " 'Foes' staggered the loyalists, 'Michael Forth' frightened them away, and 'Sweet Rocket' was exploded, a graceful gesture, with no one to see."[5]

II   Michael Forth (1919)

The problems which made *Foes* fail as fiction were magnified in *Michael Forth*. Told in the first person by the protagonist named in the title, the novel is an autobiographical narrative of events and influences in the life of a Southerner, reared during Reconstruction, who becomes an engineer, explorer, writer, and, most importantly, a mystic. Almost totally lacking in conflict or coherent design, the narrative is unified only by the progressive education of the protagonist into the world of "heightened consciousness."[6] The content is partly a catalogue of the travels and experiences of the narrator, some of them outrageously improbable and unintentionally comic, but mainly a succession of mystical experiences and conversations about the evolving universe, interspersed with extensive descriptions of scenery. Only in the early portion, in which Johnston relies upon personal knowledge for details of the setting, does the narrative have interest.

The narrator's childhood is described as a mixture of beneficent influences. He learns patient endurance of hardships and the need to take the long view of life from relatives who have had to suffer the horror of war and the humiliation of defeat. By providing him with mystical works they encourage his love of reading and foster an interest in building and rebuilding the tangible world. In late adolescence he is briefly drawn toward some unspecified vice but finds it unappealing. He falls in love with his cousin Miriam but postpones marriage until his career as engineer is launched. Exposure to business and a transplanted Scot who has read Marx lead him to awareness of a potential new social order. During an exploratory expedition to Africa he keeps a journal and practices psychic communication, which enables him to keep in touch with Miriam and to foresee rescue when held prisoner by natives. Returning home, he publishes his journals, marries Miriam, and becomes involved with pioneers advocating new theories of social and natural science. When Miriam dies suddenly, he is not disconsolate because he rests secure in his ability to communicate with her; the book ends with their shared vision of "the unselfish life" (364).

Johnston succeeds in evoking something of the quality of life in the South during Michael Forth's childhood; references to the Literary and Debating Society, concerts, lectures, political oratory, church festivals, tournaments, and lawn parties capture a sense of the culture in which Johnston was herself reared. Later, there is an interesting contrast showing significant changes in the physical appearance of New York City. However, such material is incidental to her main purposes. Even more than in *Foes*, the setting becomes mere backdrop for the narrator's psychic experiences. Though the novel moves rapidly over three continents, the real action is to be seen as taking place in the characters' minds. Extensive and frequent descriptions of nature are used as points of departure for speculations about the essence of the universe, and its physical existence is relatively unimportant in the scheme Johnston wished to portray.

The scheme is an eclectic mysticism, a compound of her own mystical experiences and the explanations she sought in various Transcendental writers but found most notably and explicitly developed in Theosophy. The list of writers Michael Forth knows, including Whitman, Emerson, Swedenborg, Spinoza, and Jacob Boehme, shows the wide range of Johnston's interest in the subject, but remarks such as "Separation from those who are 'dead' had melted from me. Separation from those who are living I saw to be a phantasm" (260) make much of the discussion read like a fictionalized syllabus for a course in Theosophy.

Given the predilection of all Johnston's characters to discuss such propositions at length, it is not surprising that they have little individuality. They are all ethereal, undistinguishable mystics, lacking even the interest of stereotypes. Even the protagonist, though one learns, presumably, his life history, is lacking in substance, and the events of his life are not made vivid or exciting. His attitude toward such extraordinary events as capture by natives is that they are insignificant in the grand scheme, and Johnston's treatment is made to reflect his attitude. The existence of a kind of evil is acknowledged in the "sultry beauty and the ancient sea call" (192) of his cousin Dorothea, but he has long since progressed beyond "that life of old sense" (192) in which physical desire could divert him from the higher life. Absence of real conflict eliminates any sense of drama from the plot.

The most praiseworthy feature of the book is that the social consciousness developed by Johnston's protagonist extends to all races. Given the climate of the time, the book is rather forward-looking; reflecting upon his relations with his childhood playmate, the ex-slave Ahasuerus Robertson, the narrator concludes that "some day the colors of the spectrum will recognize that somewhere they really *are* together, and that there is little use in playing ostrich" (147).

Michael Forth thus anticipates a theme Johnston was to enlarge upon elsewhere, but it is subordinate, as was every other feature of the novel, to the theme of mysticism. The book baffled and alienated much of her audience. One reviewer thought it avoided foundering upon the "rocks of mysticism,"[7] but most did not agree.

III   Sweet Rocket *(1920)*

Sweet Rocket is Johnston's furthest departure from the conventions of the kind of fiction upon which her success as a writer had been built, her deepest plunge into a mysticism that eschewed the qualities which give fiction interest and vitality. *Sweet Rocket* lacks both conflict and narrative incident, and its characters are hardly distinguishable types representative of varieties of modern, progressive mystics. The book has almost nothing to recommend it as fiction, and it lost Johnston all but the most dedicated readers, for whom its appeal must have lain in sympathy with her philosophical stance, appreciation for her descriptions of nature, or, perhaps, recognition of very personal details drawn from her own life or those of her friends.

The opening scene sets the pattern for the novel; it consists of a conversation during a carriage ride in 1920 to Sweet Rocket, a plantation recently reacquired by the nephew of the owner who had to give it up after the Civil War. Hints are dropped that one may travel there by other, mystical paths, but the scene is used also to provide exposition of the characters' backgrounds. Anna Darcy, age fifty-eight and a former teacher, is arriving to visit Richard Linden, the partially blind owner of Sweet Rocket, and Margaret Land, daughter of the overseer who had owned it after the war. Margaret has been a librarian, teacher, and world traveler but now attends Richard; they are in their mid-forties and in love, but not in "the once-time way."[8] The remainder of the book consists of further introduction of residents and visitors, who spend their time in carriage rides, walks, and conversation about the beauties of nature or Johnston's theories about reincarnation and the mystical identity of all things in the universe. Martin Curtin, an old classmate of Richard, arrives saddened by the death of his brother, an aviator, but quickly begins to perceive a "wider consciousness" (52), which Margaret identifies as the "added space" (56) where one may meet the dead. The pervasive mystical influence of Sweet Rocket affects all who live or visit there. Two foresters report an experience during World War I of apparent reincarnation in which one was injured and awakened first attending a wounded warrior in the Middle Ages and then later a dead German soldier in modern times. Two visiting "intellectual radicals" (121) are able to share a visionary trip to Rome, Athens, the North, China, India, and Egypt without leaving Sweet Rocket. Even the Negro preacher "Brother Robinson" (154) has a mystical experience to share, one in which he " 'touched what it's like to be God' " (157). The book ends when Anna and Martin's one-month visit is concluded, but they promise to return, even if not physically.

The report of conversations could hardly be called a plot, though there is presumably some pattern in a few characters' growth of awareness; even this element, however, is an initiation without conflict or surprise. The primary differentiation among characters is in the few details of their backgrounds and their degree of knowledge of the mysteries of the universe. Such differences are negligible and easily overcome, for there are no skeptics in the group. All is peace and tranquillity at Sweet Rocket, a situation out of which few writers would have hoped to create a novel.

Johnston was interested in the plot and characters primarily as vehicles for exposition of her philosophy, and to have introduced conflict would have been inconsistent with the message of unity and peace. Much of the message is traceable to her interest in Theosophy, but it is again somewhat eclectic and representative of what she had gleaned from wide reading on various topics. She specifically attacks orthodox theology, arguing that Christ is a concept encompassing all humanity, and she suggests that the universe is infused with "atomic energy" (102). Both the quality of the book as fiction and the content of her philosophy may best be indicated by quoting a passage representative of the whole:

"I can see that Humanity is mastering its own organism. I see that it is lifting toward Unitary Consciousness. . . .

"All our 'movements' rush into the one. All our vortices approach with a fearful joy the Great Vortex. The Correlation will be established, the Summation made. We go to join and strengthen the Ancient Heavens. The Ancient of Days draws and redeems and fuses and Ones another layer of his being."(190)

Obviously a book consisting primarily of such statements suffers as fiction, and one must have reservations about the success of the method Johnston chose to convey her message; except to those who already understand, such abstractions must seem incomprehensible.

One is left with the impression that *Sweet Rocket* was indeed intended not so much to make converts as to appeal to the converted. The fact that Margaret Land's phrase "added space" was the title Johnston selected for the account of her own psychic experience suggests that *Sweet Rocket* is an intensely personal book, and the fact that her nephew was, like Martin Curtin's brother, killed in a plane crash is a tantalizing hint that the book is more autobiographical than evidence is available to demonstrate. A "Sweet Rocket" is listed among the contents of the garden at Three Hills, and the book is perhaps a *roman à clef* in which the friends who shared Johnston's outlook might recognize themselves, enjoy her descriptions of the pleasant countryside they had visited, and agree with her message. The point is impossible to prove, but one can conclude that it would take such a reader to appreciate the book.

Such readers were few. Whatever personal satisfaction Johnston may have derived from presenting her mystical philosophy in *Sweet Rocket* was not matched by critical or commercial success. Her partisans may have shared Wagenknecht's appraisal that the book is "a serenely beautiful summation of the highest kind of spiritual experience,"[9] but most readers would agree with the reviewer who said "there is a painful sense of strain, of feverish insistence, about this exposition of a theory of perfect peace and rest."[10]

IV *Miscellaneous Short Works*

Whether by mutual choice or necessity, Johnston's short association with Harper's was over, and she had to seek other avenues for self-expression. A second change of publishers would soon provide her with an opportunity to experiment with ways to recapture an audience for her novels, but during the interval she also had begun to reach the public through other forms. One such form was short fiction, a genre she had not attempted since the early unpublished efforts which preceded her first novel. The first story was "One Night" (1920), published in the "Blue Ribbon Fiction" section of the *Chicago Sunday Tribune*. Labeled "a fantasy," the story is set aboard a railroad train trying to make up lost time on a rainy night. The main characters are the train's engineer, John Gordon, who represents labor, and the capitalist John Douglas. Though the conflict between the two is implied and insisted upon rather than portrayed, the first half of the story builds to a convincing climax; the second half, however, would be puzzling to any reader not familiar with Johnston's philosophy. Gordon and Douglas suddenly wake to find their bitterness receding and their need for brotherhood asserted as they become one person and cross a chasm to Heaven. The reader then learns the two were the only casualties when the train wrecked.

Also puzzling is "The Tree" (1923), little more than a character sketch of a servant who takes imaginary voyages while sitting under an old tree. The action of the story consists only of the servant's giving notice when a boarder wishes to convert her favorite place to a sandpile for children; the servant is too poor to carry out her threat but has enough pride to refuse money as compensation.

Two other works, hardly short stories at all, were published in the *Reviewer*. "The Return of Magic" (1922) and "There Were No More People" (1923) are fanciful projections of the future but lack plot and present the result rather than the development of conflict. In the former, Magic personified talks with her gnome about her accomplishments in the twentieth century, such as men flying and talking over long distances, and predicts that an increase of her powers in the future will allow her even to overcome her adversary, Death. A less cheerful tone pervades "There Were No More People"; war has wiped out the human race, and, after some eons, a new conscious creature has evolved from a type of bird. Selfishness makes his prospects uncertain.

The best of the short stories written during the period is "Nemesis" (1923), a chilling portrayal of the consequences of lynching. Courageously addressing a harsh reality of her time and place, Johnston shows that whether the Negro Jim Lizard is guilty of raping and murdering a white woman is of no interest to the mob which ties him to a stump and burns him. However, the four leaders of the mob have occasion for regrets; most of the story is devoted to the aftermath in which the four develop obsessions based upon guilt. A false note is struck at the end when the murdered woman appears to her husband in a vision, but the story is powerfully effective as social comment. It was so recognized by Walter White, then assistant secretary of the NAACP, who wrote to Johnston thanking her for writing a story which makes vivid the most effective argument against lynching.[11]

Obviously the five short stories reflect Johnston's social consciousness and evolutionary mysticism, and just as obviously none of them is of very distinguished quality as fiction. When the opportunity to write novels again became available, Johnston abandoned the genre until circumstances dictated that she take it up again.

The *Reviewer* not only published some of Johnston's short fiction but also was the vehicle for other work. She was invited to write the essay that opened the inaugural issue; "Richmond and Writing" (1921) praises a city which she predicts can, despite its lack of size, provide in the future an evocative setting for the production of literature to match its illustrious history and present beauty. Also published were her two poems, "Virginiana" (1922) and "The River James" (1923), both free-verse catalogues of persons and places in Virginia's past and present. The poems are better testimonials to Johnston's love of her native state than to her poetic skill or understanding of the accomplishment of the poet she was imitating, Walt Whitman.

Another short work, the introductory historical sketch she supplied for *Historic Gardens of Virginia* (1923), similarly reflects her love of her native region but also is significant for the light it sheds upon her novels. Many passages in the fiction may be explained by her assertion that "all Virginia is a garden."[12]

The most significant of all the short works written during the period was not published during Johnston's life. The essay "Added Space," written about 1923 but not published until 1947, explains her personal history of psychic experiences. Part I characterizes the sense of heightened consciousness she felt during the period of convalescence following her serious illness eighteen years before. She says she learned "we could rise, calmly, healthfully, naturally into a sensuous perception as far richer and more satisfying than the best of our present level as that best is beyond the perception of the dullard or the animal."[13] Part II describes a later experience while walking in the woods; she felt an extension of her imaginative powers much like that attributed to characters in novels such as *Sweet Rocket*. The typescript version of the essay indicates that it was intended as the introduction to a "volume" about her psychic experiences; though that work was never written, in one sense it appeared, directly or indirectly, in many of Johnston's novels. That it began to appear less directly was one of the marks of a new phase in her career.

CHAPTER 6

Experiments and Renewal

M ARY Johnston's mystical philosophy remained an important element in the six novels which followed *Sweet Rocket*, but only in the last was it allowed to become dominant again. Instead, Johnston returned to the writing of historical fiction which incorporated some of her continuing interest in causes of this world but placed greatest emphasis upon the kinds of conflict, action, and setting that had helped establish the popularity of her early Romances of Adventure. In some respects the novels published between 1922 and 1927 constitute the least homogenous phase of Johnston's career. The subjects and settings range widely, and the novels are individually and collectively of uneven quality. But they are unified by one persistent thread, Johnston's experiments with ways to incorporate her mystical philosophy without letting it become obtrusive or dominant, and the phase clearly ended when she wrote *The Exile*.

Some of the novels represent a substantial recovery of her skills as a novelist. Carl Brandt, the editor who supervised her work when she moved to Little, Brown, and Company from Harper and Brothers, helped effect changes that rehabilitated her literary reputation. Though she never regained her audience completely, and though significant changes in the literary climate of the 1920s prevented her from receiving the quantity or kind of notice she had received in preceding decades, she did attain a modest degree of popular and critical acclaim which has been ignored by literary historians. The result is unfortunate because the works deserve notice; though flawed by some inconsistencies of purpose and design, usually proportional to the intrusion of her mysticism, they include some of her most interesting—and in one case her best— fiction.

I   Silver Cross (1922)

Silver Cross was happily received by Johnston's audience because it indicated she had returned to the writing of historical romance.

Set in England during the reign of Henry VII, it contains substantial conflict and action of the kind denied or omitted from the three novels which preceded it. It portrays the political machinations of religious establishments competing for the favor of the king, the cardinal, the feudal lords, and the increasingly influential townspeople. The Abbey of Silver Cross must find a miracle to match that of its rival, the Friary of Saint Leofric, or lose favor. The principal characters, who become the instruments and the victims of the miracle contrived, are Richard Englefield, a goldsmith who has become a monk in hopes of finding meaning in his life, and Morgen Fay, a courtesan protected by her lordly patrons and her cousin, a priest. Deceived, denounced, and pursued, they eventually find peace as outcasts through visions of "the All."[1] Though resolution of their conflict demonstrates Johnston had not lost interest in her mystical philosophy, and though the novel contains some peculiarities of style and structure, *Silver Cross* contains enough compensating virtues to make it much more successful as fiction than its immediate predecessors.

As the novel opens, the Abbey of Silver Cross has prospered materially more than spiritually and shares rule of the region with the Feudal Lord William Montjoy and the town of Middle Forest. The power of Abbott Mark and Prior Matthew is threatened, however, because their rivals have uncovered some bones which they have fraudulently called Saint Leofric's and are effecting miraculous cures. Needing a "counter-miracle" (29), and playing upon Montjoy's sincere wish for a spiritual awakening, the crafty Prior Matthew devises a scheme whereby Englefield is starved, scourged, and given a drug which "sets the fancy skipping" (85). Morgen Fay is coerced by one of her lovers, the cynical Sir Robert Somerville, to appear to Englefield as the Virgin Mary. The miracle is publicized, a shrine is built, cures are effected, and Silver Cross prospers until Morgen trips and reveals "much of apparatus" (135). When Richard tries to spread the truth, Prior Matthew has him imprisoned as a madman and Morgen denounced as an agent of the devil. Somerville fails to protect her, and she is seized to be burned. However, Master Thomas Bettany, an honest young burgher, tells her story to Richard and aids both in escaping to London. They separate for a time but are drawn together by mutual danger of exposure. Recognized in London, they begin a series of flights made necessary by repeatedly being recognized. However, they develop a sense of having been together in other times and places and grow spiritually in acceptance of the universe. The last recognition is by Montjoy, who has returned from a pilgrimage and now sees that they have attained the ideal he had desired for Silver Cross.

The nature and patterns of conflict are, until the principal characters arrive in London, skillfully plotted. Considered in the abstract, the pattern at the outset is one of developing deceit and reactions to threatened exposure. The opposing religious establishments are themselves poised as one element in a balance of established powers. When one precipitates the action by practicing deceit and thereby threatens to upset that balance, the other is free to practice counterdeceit. When, however, their status within the larger balance of church, feudal authority, and people is mutually threatened, the game of power politics is abandoned, the opponents join forces, and the pawns are sacrificed. Johnston, in fact, uses the metaphor of chess to characterize the actions of the contending parties, and their interest in the game is shown to be a craving for worldly fame rather than high ideals.

The events have greater significance, on the personal level, for the pawns. After the "miracle" has been exposed, the pattern shifts from intrigue to escape, and the action focuses upon the danger and excitement faced by two victims of the power struggle. For a time Johnston succeeds in making the series of narrow escapes contain much of the drama of her earlier Romances of Adventure.

Only in the last portion of the book does the plot suffer; the escapes become so frequent as to become monotonous, and the drama shifts to the inner struggle of the characters to identify with the universe. To Johnston's credit, the mystical element is not overly obtrusive. Given the fact that throughout the book all characters have been shown to lack, and some characters to be seeking, an ideal, mysticism is much better prepared for than in earlier works.

Johnston's development of the characters is partly responsible for the success of the plot. At least five major characters are well conceived and credibly constructed to reflect the conflicts and patterns of development. Collectively they demonstrate a cross-section of human strengths and weaknesses as each seeks to fill a spiritual void, and Johnston explores the psychology of motives behind their quests. At one extreme is Prior Matthew, who sees life as a game in which fame is the prize and self-interest the only rule for conduct. He argues that a miracle based on fraud is not mortal sin if it works. Joining him is the decadent and cynical Robert Somerville, motivated by a desire for pleasure and ease and willing to buy and sell his favors. The opposite extreme is Montjoy, whose spiritual poverty is a source of anguish so great that he is too eager to find miracles where they do not exist but so sincere that he reacts to the deception by renewing his quest. In the middle are Morgen Fay and Englefield, whose discontent becomes despair before the awakening. Morgen is shown to have bought comfort but not contentment or security with her body, and Englefield craves more than life as a monk has brought. After the crisis, both are embittered because their trust was violated, and Johnston shows that their recovery depends upon the psychologically sound assumption that they must overcome hatred and forgive those who deceived them if they wish to find peace. Thus the various motives and actions of the characters are clearly defined, consistent, probable, and humanly significant; there are no wholly miraculous transformations or settlings of accounts in the name of poetic justice, even if Morgen and Englefield are the beneficiaries of Johnston's mystical Oneness.

Concentration of the mystical philosophy at the end of the novel though, focuses unwarranted attention and—a worse fault—tends to cast doubts on her certainty about how to end the story. The repetitious series of escapes reinforces such doubts, and other elements of the novel suggest an unfinished quality. Neither the natural nor the historical setting is extensively developed, and the complicated series of conflicts and events is covered in almost outline form. The style is somewhat mannered and abrupt, a peculiarity noted by several reviewers, who mixed praise for Johnston's exploration of the "psychology of belief"[2] and her portrayal of the historical setting with objections to the style, the mysticism, and the faulty construction. *Silver Cross* is not as thoroughly developed or polished as Johnston's earlier novels, but one is inclined to overlook such faults in light of the restoration of interesting conflict and characters.

II   1492 *(1923)*

The title *1492* does not adequately represent all Johnston attempted in a novel which provides the expected biographical account of Christopher Columbus and the historical circumstances of his voyage of discovery in that year but also treats three subsequent voyages lasting through 1503 and focuses upon the events and inner experiences of a fictional character, Jayme de Marchena, who has sailed with Columbus to escape the Inquisition.

By making the novel Jayme's first-person retrospective narrative, Johnston potentially avoided some risks of focusing upon a well-known and often-treated historical figure. Unfortunately, she did not use the narrator to full advantage and also did not succeed in blending elements adapted from many of her earlier works. The novel is an unwieldy and unsuccessful mixture of romance, history, social comment, and mysticism, and an attempt to condense within about 300 pages enough conflicts, events, and characters for several novels.

As the story opens, Jayme de Marchena has to adopt the name Juan Lepe because his grandmother was a Jew and he has written something controversial in the eyes of the Holy Office, evidently an expression of his vision of a "larger Self"[3] which marks his professed Christianity as unorthodox. Seeking protection, he travels to Granada and Santa Fe, witnessing a rich panorama of diverse social classes and customs in Spain in the midst of liberation from Moorish domination and on the verge of an age of expansion. He overhears an interview in which Columbus's petition for aid is denied by Ferdinand and Isabella because he demands to be named "Admiral of the Ocean-Sea"(35). Juan Lepe needs to leave the country and, when the royal decision is reversed, decides to sail with Columbus. When fever strikes, Juan becomes the ship's physician and learns that Columbus is keeping two logs so that his crew will not learn their real destination. Arriving at San Salvador, division arises in the crew about whether to trade with the natives or just seize the fruits of the tropical paradise, especially the native women. Juan remains behind to await Columbus's return and witnesses increased mistreatment of the natives and the development of factions among the Europeans, both of which contribute to an uprising and slaughter. Reinforcements for Columbus's rivals arrive and seize power, and many incidents of intrigue and war follow. At last imprisoned for disloyalty and sent home in chains, Columbus loses power but is freed to explore. The fourth voyage is beset by bad weather, trouble with Indians, and failing ships; the queen's death removes hope of further voyages, and Columbus dies with his hopes unfulfilled. Juan Lepe, however, resolves to return to the promise of a new life in the New World.

Unifying the elements of this plot was more than Johnston could manage, even with the central perspective provided by a first-person narrator. So much space and so many events are treated that the account becomes sketchy and episodic. Johnston perceived the complex set of conflicts generated by European contacts with the New World but unwisely chose to touch briefly upon many of them rather than develop thoroughly a few; the result is more confusing than complex, because conflicts among characters are left undeveloped and threads of the plot are abandoned as new issues intrude. Even the narrator's own conflicts are left hanging; his trouble about his writing, introduced early, is never explained. Jayme de Marchena's perspective upon events does provide a kind of unity, but the effect seems more accidental than planned. Evidently sensing that an omniscient point of view would not help unify the diverse elements of the plot, and wishing at the same time to avoid the difficulties of representing the inner life of a well-known historical figure, Johnston chose as narrator a fictional character she could manipulate without regard to historical fact but whose eyewitness report would provide reasonable coherence. However, she apparently was oblivious to experiments in point of view by writers of her generation, because she shows little consciousness of the need to establish the credibility or authenticity of the narrator's account. The fact that she made no effort to explain even the survival of his manuscript reflects unfavorably upon both the consistency of point of view and the integrity of the plot.

One characteristic of the narrator contributes to a further inconsistency. Jayme de Marchena's visionary musings are obviously an expresson of Johnston's mystical philosophy, and they contribute to a confusing mixture of tones. Certainly many of Johnston's earlier works are mixtures of romance, history, and social criticism, but in some of them the elements are complementary and in most there is a balance which, if not adding to the value of the novel, at least does not detract; however, by adding the element of mysticism, Johnston weakened and confused the atmosphere of *1492*. The fictional events, including numerous chases and battles, are clearly the material she used in her Romances of Adventure. Adding factual material about the settings, in Spain, aboard ship, and in the New World, provides the realistic background characteristic of her historical novels, but, when an examination of the social effects of conquest upon both victorious Europeans and their vanquished noble savage opponents is introduced, the balance of tones becomes rather precarious. It is impossible to sustain the balance, or do justice to any of the competing tones, when they are all presented as the recollections of a narrator interested primarily in explorations of a more mystical, ahistorical experience.

The one aspect of the novel which does not suffer from an excess of ambition is the portrait of Columbus. Johnston wisely made the portrait a safe composite of stereotypes drawn from tradition. Her version portrays the explorer as uncompromising not only in his ambitious goal to find a new passage to India but also in his insistence upon recognition commensurate with the goal. His vanity is large, but it is to be seen as an index to his heroic stature. Even his craftiness is a reflection of a long-standing conventional prejudice; Jayme de Marchena says that "he was not Italian for nothing!" (74). Only two aspects of the portrait, both reflections of Johnston's mind, are unusual; portrayal of Columbus's resignation to failure is reminiscent of the qualities of heroism she found in the defeated heroes of the Lost Cause, and the kinds of visions attributed to him are slanted toward her mystical philosophy. However, neither aspect is stressed to the point that it makes Columbus unconventional.

Both the author and her reviewers were aware of the novel's defects, but reviewers were more generous in their appraisal of *1492* than was Johnston, who wrote to her friend Evelyn Thomson on 8 January 1922, that "the Columbus book draws slowly to its close. It is too long a· thing, and more sheer history than story. I am sorry that I undertook it—but there! with so many (brain) children, some of them must be dull." One reviewer thought it her best novel, even though "sometimes heavy, sometimes ragged; generally shapeless."[4] The harshest criticism was directed toward the style, which one reviewer called a "curious inspirational Babu-English."[5] The highest praise came from Grant Overton, who thought it her best work after 1918 because it avoided the excesses of mysticism.[6] Whether it actually does so is highly questionable, but it is apparent that Johnston indeed did attempt to make her philosophy integral to the story; unfortunately, that was one of too many goals she set. She deserves respect for the magnitude of her effort in *1492*, but the result justifies her own evaluation.

III   Croatan *(1923)*

Johnston returned to the earliest days of Virginia as setting for *Croatan*. Although the novel has only a tenuous connection with the history of Sir Walter Raleigh's attempt to establish a colony on the island of Roanoke, it has been cited as the first to draw upon the material.[7] The only historical clues to the mystery of what happened to the "Lost Colony" were discovery of the word "Croatan" carved in a tree and the legend of Indians with blue eyes; Johnston connects the clues with a speculative account of the settlement and destruction of the colony and the absorption of survivors, most notably Virginia Dare, the first English child born in America, into the Croatan Indian tribe. Much of the material used to develop the story resembles that of Johnston's Romances of Adventure, and the book is refreshingly free of the mysticism which had diluted the fictional effects of its immediate predecessors, but *Croatan* does not match her earlier works because it is structurally flawed. Their solid underpinning of historical fact and interpretation of events is replaced in the greater part of this novel by a fanciful atmosphere and a trite love story.

A variety of motives is reflected in the three shiploads of colonists who set forth from Plymouth in 1587, but their hopes are dashed upon arrival by the realities of the New World. Rather than getting rich, building a new life, or escaping trouble, they have to contend with fever, dwindling rations, rattlesnakes, and hostile Indians. Two ships are sent back for help, but, when the third sinks, the colonists lose the chance to escape from the consequences of warfare between the Roanoke and Croatan tribes. Fleeing to the island of the Croatans, the colonists must choose between fighting and going into the mountains to *become* Croatans. They choose to go, taking the orphaned Virginia Dare and leaving behind messages, all of them except the single word "Croatan" destroyed before the rescue ships return. Over a period of thirteen years, the colonists try to preserve English customs but become used to Indian life, especially the children, who have taken Indian names such as Bright Dawn (Virginia Dare), Golden Hawk (Miles Darling), and Eagle Feather (a Spanish boy, Ruy Valdez, whose erroneous report about victory by the Spanish Armada has persuaded the colonists no help can be expected). When tribal warfare resumes, Virginia is abducted by Shawnees, surviving only by having persuaded them she has the gift of prophecy. Both in love with Virginia, Miles and Ruy spend four years hunting her; while Miles, his leg broken, waits in a cave, Ruy finds her and contemplates taking her to Florida but quickly repents. Reunited at last, Miles and Virginia profess their love and return to their home among the Croatans.

The abrupt shift in time from the colonists' flight to their new life among the Croatans, occurring a third of the way through the novel, is a significant breaking point. It marks a change not only in time and place but also in the nature of the conflicts developed within the plot, in the cast of characters, and even in the tone. The first third of the novel is perhaps too sketchy and idealized, but it effectively establishes the nature of the colonists' hopes and difficulties in coping with the New World. Their city of Raleigh is shown to be a fragile outpost of civilization threatened by nature in the form of the elements and the Indians. The plot builds to an exciting climax in the scenes of the Indian attack, when many of the characters are killed, and in the narrow escape led by Christopher Guest. After this climax, the book portrays the simple, natural life among the Croatans as an extended pastoral idyll, marred only by regrets about a life in England the colonists could not have hoped to see again even under favorable circumstances. They attempt to preserve their heritage through adherence to such customs as performing masques and dancing about a maypole, customs one reviewer found anachronistic.[8] The center of attention shifts to a new set of principal characters, the glamorous young people, white and red, who epitomize hope for continued brotherhood. The nature of the conflict shifts also. Virginia Dare's abduction becomes the occasion for development of a quest motif featuring the conventional pursuit, narrow escape, and return to safety to be expected in a Romance of Adventure; but the primary issue becomes resolution of the potential love triangle. Her rescue from the Indians is less important than her return to Miles.

The almost-fairy-tale atmosphere is certainly not dispelled by the qualities attributed to the heroine. Having dissembled madness in order to be regarded as sacred, Virginia establishes a reputation as a prophetess among the Shawnees by consulting a quartz stone and then telling them what they wish to hear; however, consulting the stone on another occasion, she sees a vision which anticipates her rescue and later is credited with a supernatural sense of impending danger which aids her escape. Virginia Dare's supernatural powers are not, as one might expect, another reflection of Johnston's mysticism. In fact, only a few indirect references to her philosophy are to be discovered in *Croatan*—in Christopher Guest's occasional glimpses of the "eternal,"[9] in another character's sense of an "inner road!" (297), and perhaps, generally, in the stress upon brotherhood and the need for amelioration of conflict. The element of the supernatural instead is further evidence of a change from portrayal of characters and circumstances at least conjecturally historical to a fantasy peopled by the timeless characters of romance. So radical are the changes that the book is structurally unsound, almost becoming two novels loosely connected, and so shallow is the latter two-thirds that the total effect is greatly weakened. Though the novel was welcomed as a sign that Johnston had returned to the kind of novel with which she had begun her career, restraint in her use of mysticism needed to be supplemented with meaningful conflict and substantial characters before she could hope to repeat her earlier success.

IV   The Slave Ship *(1924)*

Portraying the complex conflicts of a protagonist who becomes a fugitive from bond slavery and an outcast through involvement in the transportation of Negro slaves, *The Slave Ship* is the least romantic of Johnston's historical romances. Narrated by David Scott, who has been in constant flight since early manhood because he fought against the Hanover king at Culloden, the novel is set variously in Virginia, in Africa, in the West Indies, and on board a slave ship. The novel's fictional qualities are flawed but include credible characterization, substantial conflict, and a mature probing of the personal and social consequences of slavery as an institution and a concept. These virtues help compensate for the faults and make *The Slave Ship* Johnston's most convincing exposition of her mystical philosophy and of her theories about the nature of society.

The novel opens with Scott's attempted escape from English authorities who wish to punish political opponents by making them indentured servants. Apprehended, Scott is transported to Virginia, where he suffers humiliation even though treated well by his purchaser. He is befriended by an indentured clerk, Gervaise Morrison, who wishes for socialist reforms but believes that individuals must seek contentment within themselves. Scott is not persuaded, and his vengeful feelings are strengthened when, after kissing the overseer's daughter, he is sold to the cruel Daniel Askew. Having learned by observation and experience the injustices of slavery for both blacks and whites, Scott escapes during a gale. His joy at meeting a relative who allows him to sign aboard the *Janet* at Norfolk is spoiled when he learns the ship flies the flag of the Royal African Company, but his aversion is overcome by routine work and by rationalizations offered by Captain William Bartram. Arriving in Africa, Scott meets the first slaver who enjoys his work, the factor Rathbone Lace. Lace gives Scott the slave girl Fanny and helps foster a growing insensitivity to the brutalities of the trade. Scott begins to lose his sense of guilt and revulsion for the cruelties of the "Middle Passage"[10] and becomes so committed to slaving as a way of life that he is not repulsed even by the slaughter of a shipload of slaves, including Fanny. During an interlude in Jamaica he meets a Quaker who argues that the trade can be ended, even if slavery is not, but the next year finds Scott again aboard the *Janet*. When plague strikes the ship and Bartram dies, Scott assumes command; only after two more years does he awaken to renounce the slave trade and attempt to make restitution for his actions. Now having visions which promise a greater meaning in life, he is by coincidence shipwrecked near· Norfolk and recaptured. Repurchased by his original owner, he returns, reconciled, to fill out his term.

Johnston's decision to relate events through Scott as narrator has predominately positive effects, despite one major inconsistency in the point of view. Her narrator frequently switches back and forth between first and third person, sometimes within the same paragraph, and the changes disrupt the sense of immediacy provided by first-person narration. The shifts to third person establish that Scott is aware of events to come and the overall pattern of his story, but the effect is slight and probably could have been achieved by consistent use of the first person. However, the kinds of material reported and the narrator's perspective upon his story are the same throughout, and the choice is both purposeful and appropriate. It gives coherent design and helps compensate for the looseness characteristic of Johnston's plots. If one senses that Scott's early adventures could have been reported indirectly and that the horrors aboard ship become tediously repetitious, one also may discover that the material is justifiably included as part of the pattern and issues Johnston wished to develop.

The total pattern is both broader and deeper than that reflected in Scott's moral dilemma of involvement in the slave trade. While Johnston carefully delineates the horrifying effects of the trade upon its victims, her interest in the plight of the Negro is a sign of a larger corruption in society. And while Scott's conflicts as bond slave and fugitive are substantially developed, they are shown to be struggles against more than injustices of the social order; the whole pattern also includes a struggle within himself against feelings and drives which prevent him from finding meaning or purpose in life. Johnston shows Scott learning that his conflicts with civil authority and the caste system of bond slavery are less threatening than his own weaknesses; he is as much enslaved by a craving for vengeance, by a love of ease and pleasure which takes focus in rum and sex but extends to include a sense of power over others' lives, and by a lack of positive convictions as he is by society. He learns, ultimately, that the self is a prison and that flight is a form of slavery.

The message that rebellion is fruitless, that he personally cannot change society though he does not have to cooperate with its injustices, and that society is slowly changing itself for the better is a reformulation of the insight which Johnston portrayed in the mystical experiences of others of her characters, and the manner of Scott's discovery is similar, too. Early in the novel he says, "Scots folk are liable to vision" (3), and on various occasions he sees such visions foretelling specific events and scenes he will encounter. These become more expansive and culminate in ones such as the following, in which time and space are dissolved:

I saw Earth a slave ship and the wake it made. I saw that the yoke was of self, but not forever. I felt the god bound in the human self who would one day be free. . . . (286)
I knew that God is the Whole of us. I found myself and my neighbor there and we were One. I found a greater Self—oh, a greater!—a SELF that left none out. (292)

Admittedly, words fail both Scott and Mary Johnston in attempting to convey the substance of the visionary experience, and his renunciation of the slave trade, of his selfish desires, and even of his attempts to escape his fate struck one reviewer as improbably optimistic, the sign of "feminine quality of the book"[11] However, Johnston's careful development of the larger pattern of external and internal conflicts, and her portrayal of both positive and negative influences upon Scott, carry with them a sense of conviction not present in most of her mystical novels. His choice is neither an excessively sentimental reversion to innate goodness nor a sudden conversion through mystical insight, but the quite credible, rational choice of a man who has come to a better understanding of himself. Johnston created in Scott a convincing character; so effectively did she dramatize his conflicts that her mystical philosophy is more comprehensible and better integrated into *The Slave Ship* than into any of her other novels because, paradoxically, her protagonist's actions can be explained without it. One reviewer who liked the novel better than any since her early Romances of Adventure correctly remarked that "there is every possible good reason for David Scott's point of view."[12]

Another perceptive reviewer objected to some unnecessary "tricks of style" but concluded Johnston had succeeded in "synthesizing spiritual and actual adventures in a startlingly beautiful story."[13] Though it has both, *The Slave Ship* should not be consigned to the categories of mysticism or sociology; though flawed structurally and stylistically, it has been neglected undeservedly by literary historians. Among her later works, it is surpassed only by the novel which followed.

V   The Great Valley *(1926)*

Reflecting many elements but only a few of the limitations of the subjects and modes characteristic of Johnston's earlier fiction, *The Great Valley* transcends the modes and even the limitations to become one of her best novels. The novel focuses upon the struggles of a family of Scottish dissenters searching for a home, but enlarges to encompass the conflicts of a whole class of yeoman pioneers who have moved westward during the mid-eighteenth century to occupy the Shenandoah valley, apparently abandoned by Indians. The renewal of hostilities, now identified as the French and Indian War, and especially their effect upon one woman, becomes the main narrative pattern for the novel, but the historical context provides Johnston with opportunities to develop more than an exciting Romance of Adventure. She was able not only to explore specific issues of special concern to her, such as that of religious tolerance and the introduction of slavery, but also to survey the social, economic, and political conditions of frontier life. Some infusion of her mystical philosophy and development of a melodramatic concluding sequence are not entirely consistent with the rest of the novel but should not be allowed to obscure its success in fulfilling the requirements of good historical fiction.

The quest of the family of John Selkirk for a home where they may live and worship in peace opens with the voyage to Virginia. Arriving at Jamestown, they agree to help the Irishman Colonel Matthew Burke establish a town on his tract of land in the western region called "New Virginia" and begin the arduous trip up the James River. After a few years, John Selkirk has established a home and a church, and his daughter Elizabeth has married Conan Burke, the colonel's son. However, various threats to their security arise: the rebellion at home in Scotland, the Burke family's economic losses and disputes over title to lands, and a schism within Selkirk's church because he is too tolerant of Mother Dick, an accused witch, force a decision to move farther west, despite fears of trouble with Indians. When the Indians become allied with the French and war comes, the settlers are left to defend themselves because many English troops are withdrawn to protect the coastal towns. Selkirk is killed by Indians, and the quality of life deteriorates, but, when peace seems restored, Conan and Elizabeth decide to stay. Elizabeth faces a more difficult choice after a sudden attack; one son is scalped, another is thrown over a cliff, and her last sight before being carried away is of her husband about to be tomahawked. To preserve the life of her daughter, Eileen, she becomes the second wife of the brave Long Thunder and bears him a son. When opportunity to escape arises, she leaves the infant behind and sets off with Eileen and Mother Dick to make the hazardous journey back across the mountains. Her accumulated sufferings have not made Elizabeth bitter, but rather have taught her that hatred even of Indians is self-defeating. Her courage is rewarded when she and Eileen survive the journey home and learn that her husband has been rescued.

Despite some flaws very characteristic of Johnston's work, the elements of fiction used to develop the narrative of the Selkirk family clearly place *The Great Valley* among the best of her novels. The plot shares with those of her other novels the disadvantage of being too large in scope, yet the focus is sufficiently restricted as to provide more unity and coherence than in many of them. So well foreshadowed is Selkirk's death that the shift of focus to Elizabeth is neither startling nor illogical. Some subplots and narrative threads impossible to represent adequately within a plot summary, such as the involvement of two of Selkirk's sons in crucial enterprises of the New World, land ownership and the law, add density to the narrative and are well integrated with the main line of development. While the Selkirks' quest is by definition adventurous and the events of their lives the material of melodrama, Johnston's treatment of the subject matter is, throughout most of the novel, not marked by romantic excesses. Rather, most of the narrative is slow paced and well under control, and the Selkirks' story is skillfully used to develop the larger historical context.

The characters in the novel are, with the exceptions of the well-particularized John and Elizabeth Selkirk, static and undeveloped; but if they have little more depth than the stereotypes of her earlier work, they nevertheless are not conventional clichés. Johnston's interest was in developing an honest but sympathetic portrait of a representative family of outcasts forced by circumstances to settle in the mountains of Appalachia. The society which evolved as a response to conditions placed a premium upon qualities of strength, endurance, and self-sufficiency, qualities of which the Selkirks are emblematic. Johnston shows that it was an unsophisticated and yet a stable society, preserving customs and values of an earlier age. The characters are convincing as portraits of the forebears of a region which remains even in the twentieth century relatively untouched by civilization, and it is doubtful that Johnston could have accomplished this if she had focused upon individual personal conflicts.

Other fictional aspects similarly reveal flaws that are characteristic yet not as serious as in earlier works. For example, Johnston's omniscient narrative voice shows no evidence of sensitivity to the need for maintaining a consistent distance from the material; yet the narrator does not intrude upon the action. The tone shifts toward melodrama in the concluding pages, yet the change is not substantial in degree and perhaps not unwarranted by the material. On balance, both because there are fewer and less serious flaws and because there are positive virtues as well, the fictional elements alone make *The Great Valley* one of the best of Johnston's works.

The concluding sequence of capture and escape is the basis for most, but not all, reservations about the success of the novel. In a perceptive and generally sympathetic review of *The Great Valley*, Stephen Vincent Benét objected that the conclusion reflected a confusing mixture of the methods Johnston had used in her historical romances and in her more recent works, but also that "an odd air of unreality pervades the entire novel, in spite of Johnston's evident and careful researches," and that having the settlers warned by the young surveyor George Washington was "highly unnecessary."[14] Obviously the use of Washington as a character was a questionable decision because it reminds one of similar devices employed by numerous writers of the Romance of Adventure to lend some air of authenticity to novels otherwise totally lacking in reality. Just as obviously, however, Johnston did not use Washington as a substitute for development of substantial historical reality. Rather, what Benét identified as an "odd air of unreality" is the result of Johnston's attempt to invest her characters with mystical insight and a view of reality which extended beyond their time and place. John Selkirk and Elizabeth have visions in both the literal and figurative sense, and a reader familiar with the development of Johnston's philosophy would have little difficulty recognizing the specific source for the consequent air of unreality. While not subtle, her use of mysticism is relatively restrained throughout most of the novel, becoming most evident in the melodramatic conclusion when Elizabeth is drawn by forces outside herself. If not excusable, it is explainable as part of the context of Johnston's work rather than as clumsy plotting or characterization.

In one sense, the mystical philosophy is an integral part of the novel; it reinforces the theme of tolerance which pervades it. And dominance of this theme in turn may partially justify the melodramatic conclusion, for, if Johnston wished to establish the full dimensions of forgiveness and endurance of which one who espoused her philosophy must be capable, then Elizabeth's experiences are a revealing model. The gory details of slaughter, the atmosphere of danger and suspense, and especially the fulfilled threat to Elizabeth's sexual integrity certainly shift the tone, but they are appropriate choices to bring to a climax the pattern which has been building throughout. Her journey through the mountains is a logical, though considerably intensified, extension of the journey motif with which the novel began, and her ability to forgive her persecutors is an exact reflection of the message her father preached.

Certainly the melodramatic conclusion is not inconsistent with the historical context. Tales of capture by and escape from Indians have become a part of American folklore and have taken on the characteristics of myth, but they often are based upon actual incidents the circumstances of which seem less probable than fiction. Experiences similar to those of Elizabeth did occur, and, whether or not Johnston had in mind a specific story as source material,[15] it seems unfair to object to melodramatic treatment of material that is inherently melodramatic.

The greater part of the novel does not require justification, and its success is more than that of fiction alone. Before the melodramatic capture and escape sequence begins, *The Great Valley* matches the achievement of Johnston's historical novels through its serious portrayal of both verifiably accurate details about the conditions of pioneer life and the extent to which individuals are subject to the influence of circumstances. The physical setting is a significant part of the frontier experience Johnston describes. Her treatment ranges from the obvious influence of weather conditions upon survival to the more mundane but important reality of the effects of poor road conditions. More important is her desire for authenticity in treating the cultural setting, demonstrated especially by the care with which she portrayed the kinds of people and quality of life on the frontier. Her panoramic view of frontier culture included not only the sturdy, decent common man, who, lacking the advantages of wealth or connections, wished to establish a home through his own labor, but also a variety of outcasts subject to most of the vices one might imagine. Her treatment includes some scenes calculated to display contrasting facets of frontier life. The more attractive side is shown by a scene at church, where the emphasis is upon earnestness, sobriety, and hope, and the seamier side by Court Day with its haggles over property, prosecution of thieves, and drunken brawls. Always present, whether as apparent friend, harmless nuisance, or potential threat, is the displaced original inhabitant, the Indian.

Before the crisis in which they are decimated by Indians, the Selkirk family face a fundamental conflict which integrates the historical background with both the fictional plot and Johnston's philosophical beliefs. The conflict grows out of the fact that the Selkirks are dissenters in a day in which religion is taken seriously and one's choice of belief has political, social, and economic consequences. However, for the Selkirks the conflict is deeper than controversy over particular doctrines or sects; John Selkirk preaches a message of love, tolerance, and brotherhood which embraces all men, and he discovers that his neighbors are no more receptive to the concept of tolerance than were those who have made them outcasts. The Selkirks' vision of a community living in peace, harmony, and freedom is out of time and out of place; the victims of pettiness, superstition, and distrust, they are driven beyond the safety zone. Suggesting that early settlers' intolerance added to the hazards of the physical and cultural environment, Johnston develops one of her most convincing expositions of the need for tolerance.

The Great Valley is the most successful blend of the various subjects and modes Johnston attempted during the second half of her career. Even the conclusion of the novel, however much it alters the pace and tone, is not entirely inconsistent with the message, structure, and context. The fictional plot and characters work well with both the larger themes and the historical background to produce one of Johnston's best books. Reviewers, attempting to reconcile it with what she had attempted in earlier books, were generally sympathetic, calling it, for example, a "labor of love, deeply felt and sincerely wrought."[16] Regrettably, neither the popular nor the critical response was sufficient to encourage Johnston to continue writing with the restraint and maturity of judgment displayed in *The Great Valley*, and only a few isolated notices, such as the obituary which called it "still the best story of Indian captivity and escape,"[17] have given her credit for its achievement.

VI   The Exile *(1927)*

After the steady recovery of her talents as a historical novelist, most evident in *The Great Valley*, which precedes it by one year, Johnston's next work is a disappointing reversion to the matter and manner of the works dominated by her mystical philosophy. *The Exile* is an anomalous work. Unlike all Johnston's other novels, which have a clear and often substantially developed historical setting in time and place, *The Exile* is set mainly upon the imaginary island of Eldorado during an unspecified year, "nineteen hundred and blank (it will not be otherwise named),"[18] when another general war has "followed the general war of the second decade of the twentieth century" (17). While writing about the future may have offered Johnston the opportunity to show the fruition of the evolutionary progress in which she believed, the medium proved unsuccessful as fiction or exposition. *The Exile* is saved from being her worst novel only by the existence of *Sweet Rocket*, the work it most resembles.

The book opens with a description of the geography and history of Eldorado. The island was settled in the seventeenth century by a shipwrecked load of religious dissenters bound for America and has developed as a self-contained community with only limited contacts with the outside world. Traditionally it has served as a place of exile for ideological rebels, and the principal action of the novel involves the one-year exile of Richard Kaye, a radical seeker after truth who has been exiled rather than executed by the dictator George Weld, who has come to power to restore stability to a society threatened by war. The year is, by most standards, uneventful. Kaye lives in the home of Leonidas Rainbird, the previous exile, and spends most of his time in walks about the island and in conversation with other characters. He acquires a pup, a cow, a hive of bees, and a servant, whose departure and return provide narrative reference points but little relevance to the story. Kaye is mildly pursued by one woman, Julia Carlisle, and feels attraction for another, Naomi Thorne, but love in the novel is of an otherworldly variety. Some drama is provided by a crowd of boys who stone Kaye, by a storm, and by news of "dire war" (243), the outcome of which frees Kaye to return home. The real drama is supposed to occur within Kaye; he moves from a mood of despair and futility through a series of awakenings and heightened perceptions which coincidentally end both his psychological and his physical exile.

The nature of Kaye's experiences and the knowledge he acquires directly reflect Johnston's mystical philosophy. While the book at least tacitly argues against war and abuses of the social and political order, and while it seems responsive to and remarkably prescient about ideological and social conflicts which indeed led to another general war, it emphasizes three aspects of her thought: the inevitable evolutionary progress of the social order toward peace and unity, the heightened powers of perception available to persons further along the scale of evolution, and especially the specific perception of experiences remembered from other lives. Reincarnation is a persistent theme; at the time of his mood of despair Kaye senses the presence of Rainbird, and he later feels an affinity toward "James Murray, schoolmaster" (196), one of the original settlers. His relations with both Naomi and Julia awaken a sense of memory. When he sees Naomi, "once more there flowed upon him that sense of timelessness and vast, united life" (101). In the crucial scene in which he refuses Julia's offer of love, it is clear that both are reliving past experience; she says she hates and wishes to harm him and may kill herself, all as she has done before, but she has progressed to the point that the threats are not carried out. The happy conclusion Johnston projects is that in this reincarnation the characters may have found a new sense of community from which there will be no more exiles.

The essence of the manner of the novel is designed to support the message. The book is hardly a work of fiction at all, lacking conflict, incident, and characterization of any but the most elementary kind. It consists mainly of quiet conversation and sober reflection upon the points of the message. Even Kaye's anguish as an exile is mild and underplayed; it is quickly dissipated by his new powers of perception and the beauty of the natural surroundings, which Johnston as usual takes care to describe in detail. Eldorado is a pastoral, idyllic paradise, both a remnant of the past and a vision of the future, a place which will remain isolated from the rest of the world until that world reforms. Given this subject matter, both the dialogue and the efforts to represent Kaye's thoughts could not be called unrealistic, but the vagueness and abstractness of the message would leave bewildered all but those readers who shared Johnston's belief. The consensus of reviewers was expressed by one who said it contained "high thoughts and lofty visions, but difficult stuff to embody satisfactorily in the form of fiction."[19]

Surely Johnston could have had no illusions that the book would have wide popularity, and it evidently was written for an audience of believers. Her omniscient author's addresses to the reader are packed with indirection, understatement, and allusions, and this peculiarity of the narrative voice suggests a very special readership. External evidence of letters to her friend Evelyn Thomson and the fact that she was host to the traveling Hindu mystic and Theosophist J. Krishnamurti in 1926 confirm that Johnston maintained contacts with a group of fellow mystics throughout the years when she had incorporated her philosophy with some restraint into historical fiction. *The Exile* seems designed to suit her own preferences and those of her readers who would have preferred more *Sweet Rockets*.

CHAPTER 7

Nostalgia

A LTHOUGH the works which preceded *The Exile* had received modest praise and had helped recover part of her audience, Mary Johnston was resigned to the fact that what she was interested in and capable of writing did not fit the literary climate of the 1920s. She was not discouraged from writing, however, and *The Exile* may be seen as evidence that she henceforward would write to please herself. After 1927, economic constraints dictated for a time the mode of publication; she found it much more profitable to write short stories for popular magazines before returning to the three novels of the last phase of her career. The subject matter of all the works was distinctly her own choice. It reflects many of her continuing concerns and a few new interests but focuses in the best works upon that part of the past with which she was personally familiar. Obviously less interested in melodramatic action or conflict, she wrote quiet, reflective works which evoke a sometimes fanciful, often picturesque, and almost always nostalgic view of that past. If the works are not among her best efforts in fiction, some are nevertheless valuable for the insights they provide about the cultural context they portray.

I *Short Fiction*

From 1928 through 1935 Mary Johnston published sixteen short stories and evidently had plans for several more; her papers include a thirty-six-item list of "Potential Titles for Potential Short Stories." Ten were published in the *Ladies Home Journal,* two in the *Virginia Quarterly Review,* and the other four in *Bookman,* the *Pictorial Review, Harper's,* and the *American Magazine.* All but two appeared from 1928 through 1930, years in which no novel was published, and they produced in 1928 and 1929 her greatest income since 1915.

The published stories vary in quality but tend to reflect a few basic patterns of subject matter and form. Some simply resemble the sentimental, trivial fantasies of popular magazine fiction. In

"The Angel" (1929), a family recovers from poverty because they discover their painting of an angel is the work of an unspecified great artist; in "The Attic Room" (1935), a deaf elderly lady merely tolerated by her family becomes a noted poet. Johnston's interest in reincarnation and evolutionary mysticism lies behind but is not clearly realized in the supernatural aspects of "Black Lace" (1928), "Doctor Barbary's Vision" (1930), "The Buccaneer" (1928), and "The Two Business Men" (1928). The latter has some touches of humor in a spirit's comments upon how difficult it is to materialize to a person who isn't receptive. Humor is the dominant tone of "The Church Festival" (1929), which is less a story than a gently satirical yet nostalgic view of village life. At the end, townspeople transfer their optimism over prospects for a new railroad into hopes that foreign missions thus will profit and heathen gods be vanquished.

Humor also was evidently one of the purposes for a series of eight stories which feature black characters. Regrettably, the humor lies partially in the use of racial stereotypes. Petunia Sandys, in "That Cold" (1929), epitomizes the devious, shiftless servant as she provides herself a holiday by pretending to be ill. The superstitious simpleton is portrayed in the misadventures of the servant William in "If a Weasel Crosses Your Path Turn Back" (1933); sent on a trivial ten-mile journey, he suffers various physical discomfitures after meeting a weasel and is at last chased by the "father of all the weasels" and a "ha'nt."[1] In "The Mockingbird" (1928) Vinie Doane uses voodoo in an attempt to frighten her rival for the affections of William Easter.

If these stories now seem embarrassingly patronizing in their attempt to find humor through portrayal of blacks as selfish, ignorant, and superstitious, they may be explained, if not excused, by recognition that Johnston was mirroring the cultural climate of her day. If no better, neither were they worse in this respect than the Negro dialect stories of American Local Color writers. Moreover, some are rescued by the fact that the humor enlarges to express a basic sympathy for the characters and an awareness of their human dignity. In "The End of the World" (1930), the primary tone is sympathy for the plight of the preacher Vowed-to-the-Lawd Jordan and his followers, who have given away their worldly possessions in anticipation of an apocalypse he has predicted. Similarly, the comic scheme of Ailsa Craigie to win the Reverend Boykin in "The Baptizing" (1929) takes a serious turn; she is too sincere in seeking

God to pretend that she has been saved in a revival. The point of "After the Storm" (1930) seems to be that blacks such as the maid's assistant Pallas, though ignorant and incongruously imitative of white culture, deserve respect. The circus owner Moriarity's comment in "Lion Loose!" (1930) that Juniper and Rhoda must be Irish because they have been so brave in facing an escaped lion humorously makes Johnston's point; they indeed are human. "Buried Silver" (1929) contains little humor, instead portraying the loyalty and honesty of the ex-slave Dauphin, who restores the fortunes of the family he served when he recovers his memory about the location of silver buried during the Civil War.

None of the stories about black characters succeeds well as fiction, but collectively they have value as the nostalgic impressions of a woman who knew and loved black servants in her childhood. Johnston wrote to Carl Brandt, 8 December 1932, that "they constitute a sympathetic study of the Negro from a different approach." Their literary merits lie chiefly in the accurate recording of surface details, but the better ones probe beneath the surface to expose the essential humanity of the subjects.

The most interesting of Johnston's short stories is "Elephants through the Country" (1929). The story portrays what appears to be an irrational fear of elephants on the part of a backwoods mill operator, Norman Manners. He dreads the arrival of a circus featuring "Shiva The Big Elephant" and considers various measures to avoid it; his anxiety increases when he learns the circus will pass near his home on Last Mountain, but he also develops a compulsive need to "placate"[2] the beast. The conclusion is startling but inevitable; he brings about the realization of his worst fears when, trying to feed the elephant, he is seized and thrown over a cliff. The story has interesting psychological implications and perhaps is one Vernon Loggins had in mind when he made reference to Johnston's "recent Freudian short stories."[3] Whatever her inspiration, the story certainly displays compulsively self-destructive behavior. If most of Johnston's short stories are of interest only to students of her career rather than to literary critics or historians, who have largely ignored them, "Elephants through the Country" is perhaps an exception which deserves more attention.

II Hunting Shirt (1931)

Though containing some detail about life in the Virginia mountains during the last quarter of the eighteenth century, *Hunting*

Shirt is in both substance and structure less historical fiction than romance. The principal character is Alastair Ross MacLeod, called "Hunting Shirt" because of the garment he has always worn, and both the content and form of his story have a timeless quality suggesting that he is as much a medieval knight as a hero of the American frontier. To secure the favor of Myra Fontaine, he goes upon a chivalrous quest through dangerous territory in order to recover Myra's necklace, which had descended from her great-great-grandmother "that was a lady in France."[4] To the conclusion of the familiar pattern of ordeals and tests Johnston adds an innovative twist: her hero's primary gain from the quest is insight into Johnston's concept of brotherhood.

Myra's garnet necklace was lost during an Indian attack in which Hunting Shirt was wounded by Fire Tree, his Cherokee counterpart, who has found and is wearing the necklace. Hunting Shirt resolves not to see Myra again until he has recovered it. The first ordeal of his quest is living in a cave for a month after breaking his foot; during this time he sees an *"apparition"* (81) of his enemy and writes a message on the cave wall. Another test is wintering in the cabin of Job Pedlar and his three daughters, one of whom wishes him to stay permanently. Braving the February snow to escape, Hunting Shirt reaches a ranger outpost in time to participate in a fight with the Shawnees, now at war with the Cherokees. Realizing Fire Tree will have gone south, Hunting Shirt travels to the area of the Tennessee River, where he meets Niketha, who is the white woman Marian Darke. She has been reared by Indians after being captured· at age twelve and acquaints Hunting Shirt with Indian ways. Following Fire Tree into the Carolinas, Hunting Shirt at last finds him. Rather than fighting, they sense mutual brotherhood, and Fire Tree willingly gives up the necklace. Retracing his steps, Hunting Shirt is again offered love by Pedlar's daughter and visits the cave to inscribe a message of brotherhood for Fire Tree. When he at last reaches home, he learns that Myra has agreed to marry Hildebrandt Hite. Not disconsolate, Hunting Shirt decides he is in love with Marian and goes to find her.

On the surface it appears that Johnston intended that *Hunting Shirt* be read as a simple, romantic fantasy of idealism, adventure, and love; close analysis does not reveal much of significance beyond its value as entertainment. It lacks the burden of ideas imposed upon most of her works. Though the visions seen by various characters may reflect Johnston's mysticism, her mystical philosophy appears only indirectly; Hunting Shirt's lesson about the possibility of brotherhood between Indian and white does not depend upon that philosophy as source. Certainly the story implies little criticism of society. There is some apparent sympathy for Job Pedlar and his family because the harsh conditions of pioneer life have made them little better than animals, yet the characters are introduced mainly to show a trap Hunting Shirt must avoid. The opportunity to criticize established society is available in Myra's decision to marry Hildebrandt, but Johnston does not use it. Neither does she supply the groundwork of historical fact nor the sense of characters governed by their times which characterized her best historical novels. There is an abundance of detail about the natural scenery, but the main impression is that the story could have taken place at any time, anywhere. The messages of the novel, if any, are the conventionally sentimental ideas that there is good in all men, that the march of civilization into the wilderness is not necessarily an advantage, and that love will triumph.

Clearly, then, *Hunting Shirt* most resembles the type of novel with which Johnston began her career, and it resembles the type more than it does the early novels she actually wrote. It has most of the liabilities of the Romance of Adventure without the compensating virtues her early works contained. The plot is built out of coincidences that defy probability, and the characters are idealized far beyond human possibility. Potential dramatic conflict is made anticlimactic when Fire Tree readily surrenders the necklace and Hunting Shirt too easily switches his affections to Marian.

Perhaps *Hunting Shirt* was Johnston's nostalgic attempt to avoid criticism levied against all but her earliest works by returning to the mode which had made her a popular author, and indeed the book avoids many of the bases for such criticism. However, it is doubtful that popular success would have followed even if she had matched the achievement of those works, and the point is moot because, as reflected in the judgment of one of the kindest reviews, *Hunting Shirt* is a "sentimental, undistinguished tale."[5]

III   Miss Delicia Allen *(1933)*

Miss Delicia Allen is a loosely structured biographical novel about a daughter of antebellum Virginia. The account covers about twenty years of the heroine's life, beginning in 1844, when she is age nine, and continuing until mid-1863. If Johnston's novels were often episodic and disconnected, the form she chose for *Miss Delicia Allen* compounds the problem; Delicia herself is the only central focus for the book, and the structure is thus as discursive as that of *Michael Forth;* moreover, the latter portion consists mainly of letters. The main issue is how Delicia will spend her life, which becomes for a person in her circumstances the question of whether or not she will marry. The pattern of hope, disappointment, and resignation in her life is echoed in the background of events. Though Delicia spends a few years in England, the primary setting is Virginia, and Johnston's real interest, and the major success of the book, lies less in her main character than in delineation of the history and culture which produced her.

The story opens with scenes and events designed to display the various formative influences at work upon Delicia. She listens to the reading of romantic novels, wanders amid the beautiful countryside, attends church, is tutored at home, plays with the young Murray Seaton and with slave children, and talks with her kindly grandfather. Her father's death in a duel jeopardizes her situation, but the family's main fear is that she has become so accomplished a young lady that prospective husbands may be frightened away. During three years in England she meets Tennyson and becomes a social success. Her family wonders if she will marry Ralph Sidney, a young man from Richmond, but she has fallen in love with the poet Clement Aylmer. He shares her feeling, but she learns that he already has a wife and child. Preparing for a life of unrequited love, she suffers even more when Aylmer dies suddenly. Having returned home, she engages in various correspondence about the developing war, whose course through the disasters at Gettysburg and Vicksburg is reflected in the letters which comprise most of the latter portion of the book. For Delicia, the crucial news is that her childhood companion Murray Seaton is a prisoner; she now realizes she loves him, and the book ends with his return.

Of the three parts into which the book seems to divide—childhood, romance, and war—the first is by far the most interesting. As in *Hagar,* Johnston evidently drew upon the details of her childhood to provide a portrait of growing up in Virginia. Some of the experiences of the schoolroom, by a river, and in the law offices of Robert Seaton are very much like those described in her diaries. It is tempting to speculate whether other aspects of the story, such as the unhappy romance, may have had autobiographical origins, but there is no evidence to support the connection. Whatever the source of Johnston's material, this sketch of life in antebellum Virginia is the most successful feature of the novel.

The quality of life is exceedingly pleasant, and the book could be characterized as simply a nostalgic memorial if one could ignore the existence of slavery. However, Johnston does not ignore it, and her attempts to show how Delicia responds to it become an important issue. Delicia is distressed when told that she has grown too old to play with slave children and begins to be repelled by the idea that constitutional guarantees of freedom do not apply to all persons. She has developed a special fondness for her neighbors' slave, Roxy, who rescued her when she was in danger of falling from a tree. She insists that Roxy be purchased for her and eventually carries out a plan to free her. At various points throughout the novel Johnston uses Delicia to show that many persons in the South had sympathy for the Negro and would willingly have abolished slavery if it could have been done without a cataclysmic disruption of the social order. Reflecting sympathy for the plight of slaves—which is evident in her short fiction—and her earlier preoccupation with causes, Johnston's awareness and treatment of the moral dilemma, if not deep, at least probes beneath the surface of the life described.

The portion devoted to Delicia's childhood has a vitality present in the rest of the novel only when Johnston similarly evokes a picture of the cultural background, such as her description of winter customs on a Virginia plantation. When the narrative is replaced by a series of letters, the structure becomes a bare outline of battles won and lost, supplemented by description of such hardships as scarcity of supplies and medicine.

Characterization is little more successful than the plot. Though the whole novel is, in one sense, devoted to the development of her character, Delicia is not really convincing except in the early portion. Johnston shows, through incident, Delicia's childhood innocence, good sense, daring, and sympathy; her later development as a capricious, headstrong, reticent, frank, proud, ambitious, unselfish, even coquettish young woman is reported by authorial summary. Neither the substance nor the style of her letters distinguishes her from other writers, and the reader is left to guess at the feelings which led her to love Murray.

Emotion is withheld or restrained throughout the book. While the quiet tone may belie the dramatic events which form the background, it appropriately matches the lessons of silent suffering that Delicia must learn. Her life is full of promises and hope unfulfilled, but she must learn to "despair of nothing."[6] The intellectual and emotional state of mind she must attain is a reflection of the side of Johnston's philosophy which stressed a kind of stoic tranquillity If it seems to occur in spite of the facts, or without sufficient explanation, it does so, according to Johnston's beliefs, because it must.

The ultimate effect, as with the plot and characters, is an unfinished quality. A chapter which appears to be little more than an outline, the resorting to letters to carry the burden of the plot, and an inconclusive ending all suggest that *Miss Delicia Allen* was published before Johnston had come to a full understanding of what she wished to accomplish. Reviewers disagreed about the success of the novel, but one identified what may account for questionable features: "she suggests one who, having written much, has become wearied and so begins to shorthand with the beautiful facility of long years of practice, instead of enduring the patient, slogging work of changing and rewriting."[7] Johnston's own appraisal confirms the explanation; she called the novel "the simplest kind of unambitious story. I haven't felt much in the mood of writing this year. And the book market is so bad that the return whatever one does is not large."[8] In her next novel, she made a more substantial effort.

IV Drury Randall *(1934)*

Drury Randall is in many respects similar to, but a more developed version of, *Miss Delicia Allen*. The setting is again Virginia, but the time ranges from 1834 to a few years after the Civil War. The structure is basically a biographical narrative, organized loosely around major episodes in the life of the principal character. The conflicts, in both his private and public life, are similar to those of Delicia Allen, but they are larger in scope. There is a crisis in his romantic life, but he also must choose a career. He becomes a newspaperman and, while his interests lie primarily in philosophy and poetry, is forced to confront not only the issue of slavery but the larger issue of secession. His reaction to adversity also leads him to adopt Johnston's philosophy of tranquillity, but the issue is more in doubt and more extensively treated. And, despite the greater development of incident and character, the most interesting feature of the book is its display of the background of Drury's life.

The first episode described is Drury's religious conversion at age

twelve, under the influence of his Aunt Patsy, during a Baptist
revival. His father, a freethinker, protests, and a wise minister urges
that Drury spend a day in the woods to test his faith. Under the
influence of nature, Drury decides not to be baptized; the religious
faith he feels then and throughout his life is broader than that of
any particular sect. The next episode encompasses his years at the
University of Virginia; his life wavers between quiet, contemplative
study and carousing with dissolute comrades. A visit after gradua-
tion to Outermost Island on the Eastern Shore makes him acquainted with the "unearthly"[9] Rachael Gilbert, whom he courts
and marries. Assuming responsibility for the cultural side of his
father's paper, he acquires a family and a reputation as an essayist
and poet. During various travels he expands his vision and meets
Emerson, Thoreau, Hawthorne, and Alcott. A sudden hurricane
during a vacation at Outermost brings disaster; Rachael and the two
children are drowned. Time brings intellectual solace, but Drury
does not begin to feel reconciled until the death of his Aunt Patsy.
During her last weeks she softens, and, as Drury attends her, he
begins to eschew self-pity. Another dilemma arises as war approaches; the Randalls' *Herald* is loyal to the South but opposes
slavery and secession, a position that jeopardizes its future. Drury
nurses the wounded but does not fight; his resolution not to
participate is not shaken even when the *Herald* building is burned
by a raiding party. The concluding sequence describes efforts to
rebuild amid the ruins left by war. Drury's personal reconstruction
is finally effected by Whitman, travel, nature, and his recognition
that "suffering is diminished joy" (293). He is able to face his past
by visiting Outermost and returns home fulfilled.

The novel, much more obviously than *Miss Delicia Allen*, is an
expression of Johnston's thought. The opening episode reflects her
persistent distrust of narrowly sectarian religious belief, and the
philosophy Drury adopts is clearly her own alternative. Especially
interesting are the sources and a shifting of emphasis. Though an
otherworldly, visionary quality is attributed to both Rachael and
Drury, their ability to see beyond temporal affairs and feel identity
with the universe is primarily a reflection of the idealism of
Emerson, Thoreau, and Whitman. Johnston emphasizes an optimistic acceptance and trust in the benevolence of the universe, and
when Drury tells his sister, " 'In all things I see eternal unfoldment
and the goal of it all is good' " (293), he is reflecting the message of
Transcendentalism as much as Theosophy. Perhaps the most impor-

tant idea stressed in the book is that which Drury describes to his father as war approaches:

"What I pray for is that understanding that shall light a man upon his own path and yet give no denial nor bitterness of obstruction to the paths of others. To oppose and yet not oppose—to pass the paradox of opposition." (216)

The wish for conciliation, understanding, and tolerance not only epitomizes Johnston's regrets about the war, the circumstances which produced it, and the consequences which followed, but also enlarges upon the major theme of her writing career.

Drury Randall is thus an expression of Johnston's dominant ideas, but the subject matter makes it most obviously an apology for the native region she loved. The care she lavished upon description of the natural scenery reflects a definite personal interest; for the settings of mountains and the island of Outermost she surely drew upon familiar scenes and vivid memories, such as those of Cobb Island recorded in her diaries. While descriptions of the cultural setting at no point match those of the early part of *Miss Delicia Allen*, they are more consistently good throughout. From his boyhood life hunting turkey and swimming naked, through his years at the University living near Poe's former room, visiting a "house with women in it" (53), studying "under Mr. Jefferson's Elective System" (37), and continuing into later years, when his experiences include listening to opera and hoeing corn with a former slave, Drury is meant to typify a man of his time and place.

In the success of Johnston's effort to create an impression of Drury's whole life lies a possible cause for failure of the book as fiction. The setting is evoked at the expense of characterization and narrative. Drury is certainly developed at length, but the depths are not explored fully. Suggestion of a dark side to his nature in the excesses of his university days is rather readily overcome by his meeting Rachael, and his comment that the good influences of his life have helped him overcome "the old Scorpion" (109) reports the results of a battle the reader never really sees. Most of the narrative is diffuse and anticlimactic, the pattern of conciliation requiring that the major crises be subordinate to the gains in wisdom.

These faults, when added to the familiar ideas, make *Drury Randall* a work quite typical of Johnston's career. The judgments that the novel is of interest mainly to the student of her career or a person interested in its background setting, and that it does not compel such interest through its own merits, should not be taken as an indictment of Johnston's last work[10] but as confirmation of the conclusion that her best work was completed in earlier years.

A few reviewers commented about the "other-worldly air"[11] and "curiously pallid, singularly anemic"[12] qualities, but in the literary climate of the 1930s *Drury Randall* passed practically unnoticed, a fate that soon thereafter would begin to be true of Mary Johnston's whole career.

CHAPTER 8

Responses and Revaluation

M ARY Johnston's career was characterized by both diversity and inconsistency. The general patterns of change and threads of continuity reflected in the preceding analytical chapters are certainly not an arbitrary outline of her career, but neither are they a full explanation of the complexities of works which are such mixtures of idealistic romanticism, concern for historical truth, dedication to social justice, and questing for mystical wisdom that they defy convenient classification. If many of the fictional qualities of her work are predictable, the same cannot be said about the relative emphasis upon the ideas and causes she valued most or the skill with which she would realize them.

The diversity and inconsistency of Johnston's career are crucial in accounting for the decline of her popularity as a novelist. With each change she lost rather than added readers, and her efforts to return to the modes of her early work did not succeed in reaching more than a small corps of dedicated partisans. At the same time, her popularity was a barrier to serious consideration by scholars who might have regarded the diversity of her work as a virtue. Consequently, one finds that the case to be made for her significance is more a matter of consideration than reconsideration.

I Johnston's Critical Reputation

Few writers have been unkind in their assessments of Mary Johnston's work, but literary history and criticism have not been generous in dealing with her. The popular success of her early novels was matched, and perhaps fostered, by extravagant praise in contemporary reviews, but scholarship, quite understandably, has been reluctant to echo the praise of an author whose reputation was built upon best-sellers. Contemporary reviews are suspect as indications of the merits of her works because they often reflect the taste of the audience responsible for their popularity. Many give superfi-

cial summary rather than close analysis, and the frame of reference
for evaluation often is the rather narrow context of works of similar
type. Some perceptive reviews, however, contain remarkably convincing appraisals of merits ignored by later commentators, and
even unfavorable reviews accord Johnston a status now surprising.
Taken as a whole, such reviews are good testimony to the wide
respect accorded to her in her time. If it is startling to find Johnston
compared favorably with Scott and Tolstoy, such hyperbolic praise
at least suggests that her works should not have been dismissed by
scholars without having been given close attention.

Unfortunately, as Blair Rouse has noted, "Scholarly critical study
of Mary Johnston and her work is notable mainly for its scarcity.
Most of the histories of American literature give her work only
passing, often unfavorable mention."[1] Rouse cites an imposing list
of standard works in which Johnston is not even mentioned, and his
appraisal of her treatment by others is easily confirmed. Only a few
literary historians have been openly hostile,[2] but most have been
condescending in their treatment of her. Through the brevity and
narrow focus of their attention, they have perpetuated the impression that her work is uniform and trivial. Even during her life, when
evidence which might have contradicted such a view was more
readily available, historians such as Russell Blankenship implied
that she was important only as a writer who was fortunate enough to
capitalize upon ephemeral popular enthusiasm for historical romance.[3] Other writers called attention to one phase of her career, such
as the Civil War novels[4] or her interest in woman's suffrage,[5] but
ignored the rest. Even James D. Hart's history of popular taste gives
her only part of a paragraph.[6] Such neglect evidently breeds neglect,
for two recent books which survey fiction about the Civil War ignore
Johnston's most significant works.[7] Even if lengthy or comprehen-
sive consideration by literary historians is unreasonable to expect,
one must regret that few efforts have been made to study all facets
of her career, especially the practically ignored later works, and that
the kind of consideration she had received from scholarship has
perhaps discouraged further consideration.

Only two published works stand as major exceptions to the
general neglect of Johnston's career. The first, an article by Edward
Wagenknecht in the *Sewanee Review* in 1936, categorizes Johnston's works in four stages: " 'straight' historical romances" in the
first five novels, a "sociological period" from *The Long Roll* through
The Wanderers, "three definitely 'mystical' books," and a period

of "synthesis."[8] Wagenknecht argues that the key to all her work, even the romances, lies in her idealistic spiritual quest for new forms of heightened consciousness, and he has highest praise for *Foes*. Written near the end of Johnston's life, the article offers valuable insights into individual works but, in suggesting that change meant growth, tends to overvalue the later works. His concise explanation of "the 'mystical' element in her novels"[9] is admirable but does not identify its sources.

The second attempt to survey Johnston's career, by Lawrence G. Nelson, also discusses the "visionary" quality of her work but stresses that she was "a clear-eyed realist, superbly fitted by heritage and training to re-create in tragic romance the history of Virginia and of the South."[10] Nelson believes that the Civil War novels collectively are Johnston's "best history and her finest fiction,"[11] and argues persuasively that their epic, historical, and mythic qualities transcend their faults as novels; he also discovers a valid historical perspective in much of her work.

Though not in agreement about the relative value of Johnston's works, both writers recognize merits missed by most scholars. If they leave much unexplored, especially about the quality of Johnston's works of fiction, they nevertheless deserve commendation for efforts to remedy a serious oversight by scholarship. Moreover, they demonstrate conclusively that the consensus view of Johnston's work is wrong about its uniformity and not entirely right about its quality.

II *Johnston's Significance*

Mary Johnston's works are significant in several ways. While it is unlikely that they will ever again be read widely, they have the potential to interest a variety of audiences. Historians of popular taste long have recognized the importance of the early works as reflections of turn-of-the-century enthusiasm for historical romance, and Johnston's quantitative success has been noted often. Her Romances of Adventure are indisputably significant as cultural artifacts revealing one of the enthusiasms of her day. Since they typify the vogue of historical romance while avoiding some of its excesses, they are especially appropriate examples for students of the era to consult. A similar assertion may be made about the historical significance of some of the later works. Johnston's interest in woman's suffrage, social reform, evolutionary science, religious tolerance, racial harmony, and various kinds of mysticism makes the works a good index to developing social and intellectual trends of her day. And certainly her recurring preoccupation with the history of her region provides a wealth of valuable source material far greater than has been recognized. Novels such as *The Great Valley, Miss Delicia Allen,* and *Drury Randall* provide an unusual perspective, and a generation which has slighted *The Long Roll* and *Cease Firing* in favor of Margaret Mitchell's *Gone With the Wind* (ironically published only two months after Johnston's death) in its investigations of Southern attitudes toward the Civil War has been guilty of gross oversight.

Johnston's works have significance beyond that of museum pieces or cultural artifacts. Her concerns were especially, but certainly not exclusively, those of her own day. Obviously, many modern readers share her interests in social justice, women's rights, and mysticism. Though it is problematic whether greater awareness would spark a revival of interest, such potential readers owe her at least the debt of recognition.

Moreover, her works should be recognized within the larger contexts of the ideas she developed and the literary modes she attempted. Three dominant intellectual concerns and one corollary may be isolated from the great variety of ideas present in her works, and they take focus in various traditional modes. The concerns parallel closely, but not exactly, her attitudes toward the past, future, and present. History as timeless but concluded past is the concept most important in her first and last works. The past was seen through the softening haze of memory, resulting in a nostalgic, dreamlike vision of lofty ideals and heroic action. The concept of the past was static; it constitutes Johnston's tie with the timeless quality of fantasy, myth, and indeed all Romantic literature. A second major concept grew from her hopes for the future. Represented in her central themes of the need for unselfish tolerance and the amelioration of human conflict, the concept also projects a condition of stasis, an optimistic, visionary, Utopian future. The uncompromising integrity of her ideal is admirable even if one believes she would have been better advised to choose some medium other than fiction to express it. Derived from the Enlightenment by way of Jeffersonian idealism, it became crucial as the concept which lay behind Johnston's interest in evolutionary social reform; it was then transformed from social theory into mystical philosophy. This second concept connects Johnston's work with the literature of propaganda, protest, and prophecy, with persistent strains of practical and mystical idealism throughout literature, but most particularly with her American antecedents, the Transcendentalists. A third major concept, rarely dominant in individual works yet rarely absent entirely, was Johnston's reaction to the reality which coexisted with her ideals. The concept is again essentially historical, but it recognizes history as a continuous, dynamic present in which hopes are disappointed, heroism is sometimes in vain, virtue must postpone its reward, and men must struggle against external and internal forces of intolerance, selfishness, and base passion. The concept recognized the dramatic conflict and tragic ironies of human existence, and it is evident in all the works which record not just the aspirations but the actuality of history. Its corollary, almost a fourth concept but more a result of literary method than idea, is Johnston's recurrent celebration of nature; the natural world is portrayed as beautiful and sublime, as a benevolent but often terrifying force. Johnston's works do not match the aesthetic achievements of the great historical novelists, and it is unlikely that her inductive and eclectic knowledge of models would ever have led her to develop a clear concept of historical fiction as reconstruction of the past strictly in its own terms. Her preference for ideal visions of the past and future led her to suppress, intentionally in the mystical works and too often elsewhere, her concept of the reality of conflict in nature and human affairs. However, when that concept surfaces, as in the Civil War novels especially, it compensates for many faults and links Johnston's works with the best of historical novels.

The diversity and inconsistency of Johnston's career make especially complicated a general evaluation of the aesthetic merits of her works. To find value in Johnston's works first requires some concessions to the personal and literary contexts in which they were written. Unlike many of her contemporaries now more in favor with literary historians and critics, Johnston had an old-fashioned and unsophisticated concept of the nature and purposes of fiction; her novels were written to instruct and entertain, not to be admired as works of art. What interest they have as vehicles for her ideas may very well be seen as a liability when they are evaluated as fiction, and her adoption of the mode of romance requires an adjustment in expectations quite difficult for readers who perceive the novel as a literary form evolving from a bias toward realism. Indeed many of them suffer from having an intrusive message, a problem magnified in the mystical works in which the message was itself at cross-purposes with the need for interesting conflict. And certainly many of her novels, even the ones that most thoroughly treat historical content, display the excessively melodramatic plots and the idealized, stereotyped characters of undistinguished escapist fiction.

To excuse their faults on the same grounds, however, is no more just, nor is it accurate. Even if one overlooks the faults which proceeded from Johnston's concept of fiction, one finds that objective application of conventional criteria for evaluation establishes that the works vary greatly in quality. Her lack of a sophisticated concept of fiction limits the scope of analysis to rather basic consideration; little may be said about Johnston's handling of point of view, for example, because she rarely departed from use of an omniscient perspective. The tone of her works is almost uniformly serious, relieved only by occasional touches of wry, ironic humor. The rather conventional imagery of her fiction could hardly be called symbolic. Style ranks rather low on the scale of values by which her work should be judged. Occasionally Johnston attempted to represent the language of various historical periods through archaic diction and mannered inversions, and some reviewers found these as annoying as her tendency to split infinitives and omit articles. Certainly there is great variation between the densely detailed, somewhat florid style of her early Romances of Adventure and the vague, fragmentary style of the mystical novels, but the style in each case is a function of the substance. If the mystical novels are almost literally incomprehensible, it is the message rather than the style which is at fault.

The greatest number of faults in the form of Johnston's fiction lies in overall design. Much better at posing conflict than resolving it, she often seemed to lack a consistent, unified plan for her novels; what unity and coherence may be discovered is less the result of conscious design than her having evoked generalized mythic patterns, such as a quest or journey, or having relied upon specific historical background to serve as framework. Modestly successful structures are developed in *Lewis Rand* and *The Great Valley* through the fictional plots, but they are exceptions to the usual pattern. Even the best novels are much too large in scope; their episodic quality is often the result of Johnston's having attempted to cover too much time and space and develop too many conflicts. If most suffer from having too many incidents, the opposite extreme mars such works as *Sweet Rocket* and *The Exile*. Johnston seems never to have understood the advantages of intense dramatization of a single conflict within a restricted setting.

In spite of its faults, Johnston's fiction deserves credit for some forgotten or neglected accomplishments. One of these, perhaps somewhat surprisingly, is the creation of character. Unlike other popular historical novelists, Johnston rarely introduced actual historical figures without making them integral to the action of the novel, and her best fictional characters are convincingly and logically developed and motivated even when they are static embodiments of a stereotyped or mystical ideal. The portrait of Stonewall Jackson in *The Long Roll* succeeds even by realistic standards, and some of the fictional characters display interesting versions of a valid psychological and ethical human dilemma, an internal struggle with a willful, perhaps unaccountably evil, other self. First clearly evident in *Audrey*, most fully developed in *Lewis Rand*, and central to *Foes* and *The Slave Ship*, this conflict appears throughout her works, from Maury Stafford in *The Long Roll* through the title character of *Drury Randall*. In the mystical works the conflict is used primarily as a device to demonstrate an early stage of humanity evolving toward reconciliation; at its best, in Johnston's exposition of Lewis Rand's internal struggle, development of the conflict constitutes one of her true successes as a novelist.

Johnston's most consistent success is in the development of setting. Her tireless efforts to portray accurately the surface details of the historical milieus for her novels, even in those cases in which the action and characters are implausible, resulted in an absorbing sense of time and place missing from only a few works, most notably *Sweet Rocket* and *The Exile*. Her best works, and the best parts of other works, such as *Hagar* and *Miss Delicia Allen*, contain an especially vivid portrait of the background. The natural setting was almost invariably an important part of that background. Indulging her personal interest and drawing upon her extensive knowledge, Johnston filled many pages of her novels with descriptions of the flora of locales she had visited and with descriptions of the awesome effects of natural forces. The sheer quantity of detail sometimes creates a sense of disproportion, and some of the effects are purely decorative; however, the best descriptions, in such works as *To Have and To Hold* and *Drury Randall*, function to complement a core of meaning—that human life must be related to the larger context of nature, the seasons, the alternating turbulence and serenity of the physical world. The basis for Johnston's focus upon nature may have been more intuitive than theoretical, but it led to some of the most powerful effects in her fiction.

To appreciate Johnston's accomplishments as a novelist, one must be willing to suspend absolute criteria and to accept the value of mixed successes. Readers today who are willing to approach her fiction in the context of the modes she adopted, to see beyond the barriers erected by her commitment to causes, and to be tolerant of some faults in execution will make some rewarding discoveries in the fiction of Mary Johnston.

Notes and References

Preface

1. "Mary Johnston," *New York Times*, 11 May 1936, sect. 1, p. 18.

Chapter One

1. Alice Payne Hackett, *70 Years of Best Sellers: 1895-1965* (New York: R. R. Bowker Company, 1967), p. 96.
2. Annie Kendrick Walker, "Mary Johnston in Her Home," *New York Times*, 24 March 1900, p. 181.
3. Ibid.
4. Brief biographical sketches are available in various standard references. Two good surveys are Ernest Leisy, "Mary Johnston," *Dictionary of American Biography*, ed. Robert Livingston Schuyler et al. (New York: Charles Scribner's Sons, 1958), vol. 22, suppl. 2, pp. 349-50, and "Mary Johnston," *Notable American Women, 1607-1950: A Biographical Dictionary*, ed. Edward T. James et al. (Cambridge: The Belknap Press of Harvard University Press, 1971), II, 282-84. Her family history is the focus in Philip A. Bruce et al., *History of Virginia* (Chicago: American Historical Society, 1924), IV, 9-10. More personal, anecdotal information is in four sources: E. S. Boddington, "Mary Johnston in Birmingham, Alabama," *Women Authors of Our Day in Their Homes*, ed. Francis Whiting Halsey (New York: James Pott & Company, 1903), pp. 93-99; Edward Francis Harkins and C. H. L. Johnston, *Little Pilgrimages Among the Women Who Have Written Famous Books* (Boston: L. C. Page and Company, 1901), pp. 299-313; "Mary Johnston, Writer of the Past," *Journal of the Roanoke Historical Society* 6 (Winter 1970): 17-22; and "Mary Johnston," *New York Times*, 29 March 1902, p. 198.
5. Edward Wagenknecht, "The World and Mary Johnston," *Sewanee Review* 44 (April-June 1936): 188-206, and "Allotropes and Mary Johnston," *Cavalcade of the American Novel* (New York, 1952), pp. 197-203. The latter volume is dedicated to Johnston.
6. Unless otherwise noted, throughout this study all biographical information and quoted material attributed to Johnston have been taken from the Mary Johnston Collection (accession no. 3588), Manuscripts Department, University of Virginia Library, identified as Mary Johnston Papers.
7. "Mary Johnston and the Historic Imagination," *Southern Writers: Appraisals in Our Time*, ed. R. C. Simonini, Jr. (Charlottesville: The University Press of Virginia, 1964), p. 74.

8. Her sister Anne was the only sibling who married. She married a cousin, Thomas Henry Johnston, and died April 3, 1901, after giving birth to her third son, who died nine months later.

9. "Cavalier and Indentured Servant in Virginia Fiction," *South Atlantic Quarterly* 26 (January 1927): 28.

10. Arthur Goodrich, "Mary Johnston." Obituary for "the local weekly"; clipping in Mary Johnston Papers.

11. Leisy, *DAB*, p. 350.

12. *Atlantic Monthly*, June 1899 through March 1900.

13. In addition to many personal and business letters, the Mary Johnston Papers contain congratulatory messages from many fellow authors. Some of the more interesting correspondents include Van Wyck Brooks, James Branch Cabell, Rebecca Harding Davis, Margaret Deland, Zona Gale, Ellen Glasgow, and George Barr McCutcheon. Theodore Dreiser wrote in 1910 suggesting that she supply a serial novel about suffrage for *The Delineator*.

14. "The Manuscripts of Some Popular Novels," *Critic*, December 1900, pp. 484-85.

15. "Miss Mary Johnston Outlines Her Views of Woman Suffrage," *Richmond Times-Dispatch*, 15 November 1907, p. 8.

16. "The Woman's War," *Atlantic Monthly*, April 1910, pp. 559-70. Also interesting are typescripts in the Mary Johnston Papers: "Wanted—An Architect" and "The Eugenical Point of View."

17. Trudy Jean Hanmer, "A Divine Discontent: Mary Johnston and Woman Suffrage in Virginia," M.A. thesis, University of Virginia 1972, provides an extensive discussion of Johnston's activities and stresses the importance of eugenics in her point of view.

18. "Added Space," *The Fireside Book of Ghost Stories*, ed. Edward Wagenknecht (Indianapolis: The Bobbs-Merrill Company, 1947), pp. 527-33.

19. No extensive, objective exposition of Theosophy exists, but most standard encyclopedias provide basic information. A fascinatingly biased account of the movement's politics is in Josephine Marie Ransom, *A Short History of the Theosophical Society* (Adyar, India: Theosophical Publishing House, 1938).

20. The Certificate of Death lists the cause as cancer of the kidney.

Chapter Two

1. James D. Hart, *The Popular Book: A History of America's Literary Taste* (Berkeley: University of California Press, 1961), p. 199.

2. *The American Historical Novel* (Norman, Okla., 1950), p. 18.

3. Mary Johnston, *Prisoners of Hope* (Boston, 1898), p. 248. Subsequent page references for material quoted from this edition are included within parentheses in the text.

4. Hubbell, "Cavalier and Indentured Servant," p. 35.

5. *Athenaeum*, 21 January 1899, p. 80.

6. *Atlantic Monthly*, January 1899, p. 134.

7. *Dial*, 1 November 1898, p. 303.

8. Unpublished letter to Houghton Mifflin Company, November 20, 1900. In demonstrating that the novel is not a plagiarized version of Mrs. Maud Wilder Goodwin's *The Head of a Hundred*, Johnston explains her method of developing an idea for a novel as well as the specific incidents upon which *To Have and To Hold* is based. She noted that the chronology is somewhat disrupted but claimed that the events themselves are portrayed accurately. The letter has been used throughout this discussion to explain her methods and intent.

9. William E. Simonds, "Three American Historical Romances," *Atlantic Monthly*, March 1900, p. 412.

10. Mary Johnston, *To Have and To Hold* (Boston, 1900), p. 30. Subsequent page references for material quoted from this edition are included within parentheses in the text.

11. Jeannette Gilder, *Harper's Bazaar*, 17 February 1900, p. 134.

12. Johnston's correspondence with the successful aspirant, E. F. Boddington, reveals an increasing exasperation.

13. Norman Hapgood, "The Drama of the Month," *Bookman*, April 1901, pp. 163-65. Hapgood thought the play bad because it failed to represent Johnston's greater facility with the English language than that of such rivals as Winston Churchill and Paul Leicester Ford.

14. Daniel Blum, *A Pictorial History of the Silent Screen* (New York: G. P. Putnam's Sons, 1953), p. 101.

15. A letter from Carl Brandt to Elizabeth Johnston indicates that as late as December 14, 1939, he was still trying to sell "talking rights" to Paramount, which held "silent rights."

16. Wallace Stevens, *The Letters of Wallace Stevens*, ed. Holly Stevens (New York: Alfred A. Knopf, 1966), p. 111.

17. Thomas Dixon, Jr., "Miss Johnston's Virginia," *Bookman*, November 1900, pp. 237-38.

18. Wagenknecht, "Allotropes," p. 202.

19. Stanley J. Kunitz and Howard Haycraft, eds., *Twentieth Century Authors: A Biographical Dictionary of Modern Literature* (New York: H. W. Wilson Company, 1942), p. 733.

20. Cornelia Atwood Pratt, "Miss Johnston's 'Velvet Gown,' " *Critic*, April 1900, p. 351.

21. Leisy, *American Historical Novel*, p. 27.

22. Mary Johnston, *Audrey* (Boston, 1902), p. 111. Subsequent page references for material quoted from this edition are included within parentheses in the text.

23. The production was no more successful than that of *To Have and To Hold*. A reviewer argued that its "six tableaux" omitted most of what was

appealing in the novel; see " 'Audrey' in Tabloids," *New York Times*, 25 November 1902, sect. 9, p. 3.

24. Eleanor Robson Belmont, *The Fabric of Memory* (New York: Farrar, Straus and Cudahy, 1957), p. 19.

25. A. H. Quinn, *American Fiction: An Historical and Critical Survey* (New York, 1936), pp. 502-503.

26. Harry Thurston Peck, *Bookman*, March 1902, p. 72.

27. M. Gordon Pryor Rice, " 'Audrey,' " *New York Times*, 22 February 1902, p. 123.

28. Peck, p. 72.

29. *Independent*, 20 March 1902, pp. 696-97; M. H. V., "Mary Johnston's 'Audrey,' " *Critic*, March 1902, p. 260.

30. Rice, p. 123.

31. Mary Johnston, *Sir Mortimer* (New York, 1904), p. 76. Subsequent page references for material quoted from this edition are included within parentheses in the text.

32. "Miss Johnston's Latest Story," *New York Times*, 2 April 1904, p. 224.

33. Mary Johnston, *The Goddess of Reason* (Boston, 1907), p. 35. Subsequent page references for material quoted from this edition are included within parentheses in the text.

34. "The Goddess of Reason," *New York Times*, 16 February 1909, sect. 6, p. 1.

35. *Literary Digest*, 13 July 1907, p. 62.

36. *New York Times*, 16 February 1909, p. 1.

37. *Atlantic Monthly*, December 1907, p. 849.

38. "Julia Marlowe in New Play," *New York Times*, 22 December 1908, sect. 4, p. 5.

39. "The Goddess of Reason," *New York Times*, 21 February 1909, sect. 5, p. 14.

40. *New York Times*, 16 February 1909, p. 1.

Chapter Three

1. Nelson, p. 89.

2. Sheldon Van Auken, "The Southern Historical Novel in the Early Twentieth Century," *Journal of Southern History* 14 (1948): 170.

3. A ledger book headed "March 6. 1908" contains an account of the writing of *Lewis Rand* as well as much autobiographical data about Johnston's youth.

4. *Address read at Vicksburg upon the occasion of the unveiling of a tablet commemorating the service to the South of the Botetourt artillery, by Mary Johnston* (Cambridge, Mass., [1907]).

5. Leisy, *American Historical Novel*, p. 18.

6. Ibid., p. 4.

7. Nelson, p. 80.

8. Ibid., pp. 89-102.

9. Mary Johnston, *Lewis Rand* (Boston, 1908), p. 395. Subsequent page references for material quoted from this edition are included within parentheses in the text.

10. "Powerful Novel by Mary Johnston," *New York Times*, 3 October 1908, p. 538.

11. Caroline B. Sherman, "The Rediscovery of Mary Johnston, " *Southern Literary Messenger* N.S. 4 (1942): 432.

12. "Powerful Novel," p. 538.

13. *Nation*, 1 October 1908, p. 317.

14. *Spectator*, 28 November 1908, p. 887.

15. "Powerful Novel," p. 538.

16. Leisy, *American Historical Novel*, p. 120.

17. Mary Johnston, *The Long Roll* (Boston, 1911), p. 161. Subsequent page references for material quoted from this edition are included within parentheses in the text.

18. Authors, titles, and spelling have been emended, except in quoted material.

19. "The Image of an Army: The Civil War in Southern Fiction," *Southern Writers: Appraisals in Our Time*, ed. R. C. Simonini, Jr. (Charlottesville: The University Press of Virginia, 1964), p. 63.

20. *Dial*, 16 July 1911, p. 51.

21. Nelson, p. 96.

22. Separately published in *Great Stories of the Sea & Ships*, ed. N. C. Wyeth (Philadelphia: David McKay & Company, 1940), pp. 184-98, and as "The Merrimac and the Monitor," *Men at War*, ed. E. Hemingway (N.P.: Crown Publishers, 1942), pp. 493-502. Other portions extracted were "Gettysburg," *Atlantic Monthly*, July 1912, pp. 1-9, and "Fredericksburg," *Fighting Americans*, ed. F. Van Wyck Mason (New York: Reynal & Hitchcock, 1943), pp. 501-11.

23. *The Women Who Make Our Novels*, rev. ed. (New York: Dodd Mead & Company, 1928), pp. 193-94.

24. Monroe Fulkerson Cockrell, *Stonewall Jackson: A Descriptive Study of Fourteen Pages from Books Before and a Few After The Long Roll* (Evanston, Ill.: privately printed, 1955). Cockrell compiles an array of sources which do not mention Jackson's eccentricities; their silence purportedly demonstrates that he was not eccentric.

25. "Criticism Heaped on 'The Long Roll,' " *Richmond Times-Dispatch*, 14 October 1911, pp. 1-2. The first objection, by a "Dr. Smith" on September 12, 1911, is summarized.

26. 15 October 1911, Industrial Sect., p. 4.

27. "Mrs. 'Stonewall' Jackson Denounces 'The Long Roll,' " *New York Times*, 29 October 1911, sect. 5, p. 9.

28. *Spectator*, 16 September 1911, p. 424.

29. *Baltimore Sun*, 4 June 1911 (clipping in Mary Johnston Papers).

30. *Syracuse Herald*, 5 June 1911 (clipping in Mary Johnston Papers).

31. Mary Johnston, *Cease Firing* (Boston, 1912), p. 19.

32. "A War as War," *New York Times*, 17 November 1912, p. 677.

33. Frank E. Vandiver, intro. to Joseph E. Johnston, *Narrative of Military Operations* (Bloomington: Indiana University Press, 1959), p. ix.

34. "A War as War," p. 677.

35. Robert A. Lively, *Fiction Fights the Civil War: An Unfinished Chapter in the Literary History of the American People* (Chapel Hill, N.C., 1957), p. 16.

Chapter Four

1. "Miss Mary Johnston Outlines Her Views of Woman Suffrage," *Richmond Times-Dispatch*, 15 November 1909, p. 8.

2. "Virginia's Great Colleges," *Richmond-Times Dispatch*, 10 February 1910, p. 6.

3. Letter to B. M. Dutton, ca. 1911; copy in Mary Johnston Papers.

4. Mary Johnston, *Hagar* (Boston, 1913), p. 16. Subsequent page references for material quoted from this edition are included within parentheses in the text.

5. Helen Bullis, "A Feminist Novel," *New York Times*, 2 November 1913, p. 571.

6. Ibid., p. 571.

7. 6 January 1914 (clipping in Mary Johnston Papers).

8. Nelson, p. 71.

9. Frederic Taber Cooper, *Bookman*, January 1915, p. 553.

10. Mary Johnston, *The Witch* (Boston, 1914), pp. 177-78. Subsequent page references for material quoted from this edition are included within parentheses in the text.

11. *New York Times*, 1 November 1914, p. 474.

12. *Outlook*, 11 November 1914, p. 603.

13. *Independent*, 1 February 1915, p. 176.

14. "Pseudo-Historical," *New Republic* 28 November 1914, p. 28.

15. Mary Johnston, *Fortunes of Garin* (Boston, 1915) p. 45. Subsequent page references for material quoted from this edition are included within parentheses in the text.

16. *Independent*, 22 November 1915, p. 318.

17. "Recent Fiction," *Dial*, 20 January 1916, p. 78.

18. "Mary Johnston's Historical Romance," *New York Times*, 24 October 1915, p. 402.

19. Mary Johnston, *The Wanderers* (Boston, 1917), p. 32. Subsequent page references for material quoted from this edition are included within parentheses in the text.

20. Undated copies of letters to Julia Tutwiler in Mary Johnston Papers; one reply dated 20 September 1916.

21. *New York Times*, 30 September 1917, p. 365.

22. *New Republic*, 5 January 1918, p. 291.

23. *New York Vogue*, 5 December 1917 (clipping in Mary Johnston Papers).

24. *Chicago Tribune*, 20 October 1917 (clipping in Mary Johnston Papers).

Chapter Five

1. *Dial*, 6 September 1919, p. 216.

2. "Mary Johnston's Adventures," *Cargoes for Crusoes* (New York: D. Appleton & Company, 1924), p. 381.

3. Mary Johnston, *Foes* (New York, 1918), p. 139. Subsequent page references for material quoted from this edition are included within parentheses in the text. The title of the English edition, *The Laird of Glenfernie*, was a curious choice: a novel entitled *The Lairds of Glenfern*, written by another Mary Johnston, had been published in 1816.

4. "Allotropes," p. 201.

5. "Mary Johnston," *The Literary Spotlight* (New York: Doubleday & Company, Inc., 1924), p. 48.

6. Mary Johnston, *Michael Forth* (New York, 1919), p. 248. Subsequent page references for material quoted from this edition are included within parentheses in the text.

7. *New York Times*, 14 December 1919, sect. 7, p. 1.

8. Mary Johnston, *Sweet Rocket* (New York, 1920), p. 10. Subsequent page references for material quoted from this edition are included within parentheses in the text.

9. "The World and Mary Johnston," p. 189.

10. H. W. Boynton, "More or Less Novels," *Bookman*, January 1921, p. 342.

11. Letter dated June 18, 1923; copy in Mary Johnston Papers.

12. Mary Johnston, "Introductory," *Historic Gardens of Virginia*, ed. Edith Tunis Sale (Richmond, Va., 1923), p. 16.

13. "Added Space," p. 530.

Chapter Six

1. Mary Johnston, *Silver Cross* (Boston, 1922), p. 261. Subsequent page references for material quoted from this edition are included within parentheses in the text.

2. *London Times Literary Supplement*, 15 June 1922, p. 395.

3. Mary Johnston, *1492* (Boston, 1922), p. 5. Subsequent page refer-

ences for material quoted from this edition are included within parentheses in the text.

4. Isabel Paterson, *New York Tribune*, 12 November 1922, p. 8.

5. Georgia Wood Pangborn, "New Fiction in Varied Forms," *New York Herald*, 12 November 1922 (clipping in Mary Johnston Papers).

6. *The Women Who Make Our Novels*, p. 198.

7. Leisy, *American Historical Novel*, p. 22.

8. "Latest Works of Fiction," *New York Times*, 28 October 1923, p. 8.

9. Mary Johnston, *Croatan* (Boston, 1923), p. 21. Subsequent page references for material quoted from this edition are included within parentheses in the text.

10. Mary Johnston, *Slave Ship* (Boston, 1924), pp. 167-68. Subsequent page references for material quoted from this edition are included within parentheses in the text.

11. H. L. Pangborn, "Fiction with a Feminine View-Point," *Literary Digest International Book Review*, December 1924, p. 18.

12. Emily Clark, "Africa in Exile," *New York Herald Tribune*, 7 December 1924, p.4.

13. "Mary Johnston's Novel Out of Africa," *New York Times*, 16 November 1924, p. 8.

14. "Out of Focus," *Saturday Review of Literature*, 15 May 1926, p. 787.

15. An indirect source possibly was her ancestor Charles Johnston's *A Narrative of the Incidents Attending the Capture, Detention and Ransom of Charles Johnston, of Botetourt County, Virginia, who was made Prisoner by the Indians, on the River Ohio, in the Year 1790; . . .* (New York: J. & J. Harper, 1827).

16. Isabel Patterson, "Our Fathers That Begat Us," *New York Herald Tribune*, 2 May 1926, sect. 7, p. 4.

17. "Mary Johnston," *Saturday Review of Literature*, 23 May 1936, p. 8.

18. Mary Johnston, *The Exile* (Boston, 1927), p. 15. Subsequent page references for material quoted from this edition are included within parentheses in the text.

19. *Outlook*, 5 October 1927, p. 155.

Chapter Seven

1. Mary Johnston, "If a Weasel Crosses Your Path Turn Back," *Virginia Quarterly Review* 9 (January 1933): 104.

2. Mary Johnston, "Elephants Through the Country," *Virginia Quarterly Review* 5 (January 1929): 78.

3. Vernon Loggins, *I Hear America . . . : Literature in the United States* (New York: Thomas Y. Crowell Company, 1937), p. 75.

4. Mary Johnston, *Hunting Shirt* (Boston, 1931), p. 35. Subsequent

page references for material quoted from this edition are included within parentheses in the text.

5. "Check List of New Books," *American Mercury*, January 1932, p. xxiv.

6. Mary Johnston, *Miss Delicia Allen* (Boston, 1933), p. 301.

7. Edward Larocque Tinker, "Ghosts of Gallant Heroes and Brave Women," *New York Herald Tribune*, 5 March 1933, sect. 10, p. 6.

8. Letter to Evelyn Thomson dated April 14, 1933; copy in Mary Johnston Papers.

9. Mary Johnston, *Drury Randall* (Boston, 1934), p. 79. Subsequent page references for material quoted from this edition are included within parentheses in the text.

10. *Drury Randall* was of course not intended to be her last work. She had completed at the time of her death the major portion of a typescript for "A Far Country," another novel about a seeker after mystical truth. Nothing in that projected work suggests that publication would have added to her stature as novelist.

11. *North American Review* 238 (December 1934): 574.

12. Louise Maunsell Field, "Civil War Sidelines," *New York Times*, 14 October 1934, sect. 5, p. 23.

Chapter Eight

1. "Mary Johnston (1870-1936)," *A Bibliographical Guide to the Study of Southern Literature*, ed. Louis D. Rubin, Jr. (Baton Rouge: Louisiana State University Press, 1969), p. 230.

2. V. F. Calverton, *The Liberation of American Literature* (New York: Charles Scribner's Sons, 1932), p. 111n.

3. *American Literature as an Expression of the National Mind* (New York: Henry Holt and Company, [1931]), pp. 548-49.

4. Van Wyck Brooks, *The Confident Years: 1885-1915* (New York: E. F. Dutton & Co., 1955), pp. 334, 373.

5. Vernon L. Parrington, *The Beginnings of Critical Realism in America: 1860-1920* (New York: Harcourt, Brace and Company, 1930), p. 180.

6. *The Popular Book*, p. 199.

7. Daniel Aaron, *The Unwritten War: American Writers and the Civil War* (New York: Alfred A. Knopf, 1973); Peter Aichinger, *The American Soldier in Fiction, 1880-1963: A History of Attitudes Toward Warfare and the Military Establishment* (Ames: Iowa State University Press, 1975).

8. "The World and Mary Johnston," pp. 192-93.

9. Ibid., p. 198.

10. Nelson, p. 73.

11. Ibid., p. 89.

Selected Bibliography

PRIMARY SOURCES

Books listed are the first American editions and the accompanying English editions for which a change of title was required. Serial publication of *To Have and To Hold* and *Audrey* in the *Atlantic Monthly* and *Sir Mortimer* in *Harper's Monthly* preceded the editions cited. Short stories are the first published versions; deliberately excluded are some extracts from novels occasionally indexed as short stories (see Chapter 3, note 22). Miscellaneous writings are a representative selection of published essays, letters, and speeches.

1. Books: Fiction
Audrey. Boston: Houghton, Mifflin and Company, 1902.
Cease Firing. Boston: Houghton, Mifflin and Company, 1912.
Croatan. Boston: Little, Brown, and Company, 1923.
Drury Randall. Boston: Little, Brown, and Company, 1934.
The Exile. Boston: Little, Brown, and Company, 1927.
Foes. New York: Harper & Brothers Publishers, [1918]. Published in England as *The Laird of Glenfernie*. London: Constable and Company, 1919.
The Fortunes of Garin. Boston: Houghton, Mifflin and Company, 1915.
1492. Boston: Little, Brown, and Company, 1922. Published in England as *Admiral of the Ocean-Sea*. London: T. Butterworth, Ltd., [1923].
The Great Valley. Boston: Little, Brown, and Company, 1926.
Hagar. Boston: Houghton, Mifflin and Company, 1913.
Hunting Shirt. Boston: Little, Brown, and Company, 1931.
Lewis Rand. Boston: Houghton, Mifflin and Company, 1908.
The Long Roll. Boston: Houghton, Mifflin and Company, 1911.
Michael Forth. New York: Harper & Brothers Publishers, [1919].
Miss Delicia Allen. Boston: Little, Brown, and Company, 1933.
Prisoners of Hope. Boston: Houghton, Mifflin and Company, 1898. Published in England as *The Old Dominion*. London: Archibald Constable & Co., 1899.
Silver Cross. Boston: Little, Brown, and Company, 1922.
Sir Mortimer. New York: Harper & Brothers Publishers, 1904.
The Slave Ship. Boston: Little, Brown, and Company, 1924.
Sweet Rocket. New York: Harper & Brothers Publishers, [1920].
To Have and To Hold. Boston: Houghton, Mifflin and Company, 1900.

Published in England as *By Order of the Company*. London: A. Constable and Company, 1900.
The Wanderers. Boston: Houghton, Mifflin and Company, [1917].
The Witch. Boston: Houghton, Mifflin and Company, 1914.

2. Other Books
The Goddess of Reason. Boston: Houghton, Mifflin and Company, 1907.
Pioneers of the Old South. New Haven: Yale University Press, 1918.

3. Short Stories
"After the Storm." *American Magazine*, August 1930, pp. 36-37, 139-44.
"The Angel." *Ladies Home Journal*, January 1929, pp. 10, 11, 102, 104.
"The Attic Room." *Ladies Home Journal*, December 1935, pp. 5, 6, 78, 80, 81, 83, 85, 87.
"The Baptizing." *Ladies Home Journal*, April 1929, pp. 16, 17, 91, 92, 94.
"Black Lace." *Ladies Home Journal*, August 1928, pp. 16, 17, 66, 68, 70.
"The Buccaneer." *Ladies Home Journal*, June 1928, pp. 6, 7, 68, 70.
"Buried Silver." *Ladies Home Journal*, September 1929, pp. 6, 7, 158-62.
"The Church Festival." *Bookman*, September 1929, pp. 66-72.
"Doctor Barbary's Vision." *Pictorial Review*, December 1930, pp. 10, 11, 76-78.
"Elephants through the Country." *Virginia Quarterly Review* 5 (January 1929), 59-83.
"The End of the World." *Ladies Home Journal*, March 1930, pp. 10, 11, 172, 175, 178.
"If a Weasel Crosses Your Path Turn Back." *Virginia Quarterly Review* 9 (January 1933): 87-107.
"Lion Loose!" *Ladies Home Journal*, October 1930, pp. 14, 15, 130, 133, 135, 138.
"The Mockingbird." *Ladies Home Journal*, November 1928, pp. 10, 11, 83, 84, 86.
"Nemesis." *Century*, May 1923, pp. 2-22.
"One Night." *Chicago Tribune*, 25 July 1920, pp. 1, 2, 6.
"The Return of Magic." *Reviewer* 3 (April 1922): 359-63.
"That Cold." *Ladies Home Journal*, November 1929, pp. 28, 29, 222, 224, 227.
"There Were No More People Upon the Earth." *Reviewer* 4 (October 1923): 3-8.
"The Tree." *Good Housekeeping*, May 1923, pp. 54-57, 232-34.
"Two Business Men." *Harper's Monthly*, September 1928, pp. 445-55.

4. Poems
"Bookland." *Little Verses and Big Names*. New York: George H. Doran Company, 1915, pp. 104-105.
"The River James." *Reviewer* 3 (April 1923): 850-55.
"Virginiana." *Reviewer* 5 (February 1922): 263-67.

5. Miscellaneous Writing

"Added Space." *The Fireside Book of Ghost Stories,* ed. Edward Wagen-
    knecht. Indianapolis: The Bobbs-Merrill Company, [1947], pp. 527-33.
*Address read at Vicksburg upon the occasion of the unveiling of a tablet
    commemorating the services to the South of the Botetourt artillery, by
    Mary Johnston.* Cambridge, Mass.: H. O. Houghton & Co., [1907].
"Introductory." *Historic Gardens of Virginia,* compiled by the James River
    Garden Club; edited by Edith Tunis Sale. Richmond, Va.: The William
    Byrd Press, Inc., [1923], pp. 13-16.
"Jefferson at Monticello: From an Undiscovered Diary, Midsummer 1810."
    *The American Historical Scene as Depicted by Stanley Arthurs and
    Interpreted by Fifty Authors.* Philadelphia: The University of Pennsyl-
    vania Press, 1935, pp. 114-15.
"Letter to the Editor." *Richmond Times-Dispatch,* 15 October 1911,
    Industrial Section, p. 4.
Mary Johnston to the House of Governors. New York: National American
    Woman Suffrage Association, [1912].
"Richmond and Writing." *Reviewer* 1 (February 1921): 7-11.
*The Status of Woman. A Letter to the Richmond, Virginia, Times-Dispatch,
    Dec. 11, 1909.* Richmond, Va.: Equal Suffrage League of Virginia,
    [1909].
"Virginia's Great Colleges." *Richmond Times-Dispatch,* 10 February 1910,
    p. 6.
"The Woman's War." *Atlantic Monthly,* April 1910, pp. 559-70.

SECONDARY SOURCES

See Chapter 1, note 4 for important biographical sources; other special-
ized or incidental sources relevant to individual works are listed among the
Notes and References.

COLEMAN, ELIZABETH DABNEY. "Penwoman of Virginia's Feminists." *Virginia
    Cavalcade* 6: 3 (1956): 8-11. The best published account of Johnston's
    suffrage activities, though it considers only *Hagar.* Includes illustra-
    tions.
HANMER, TRUDY JEAN. "A Divine Discontent: Mary Johnston and Woman
    Suffrage in Virginia." M.A. thesis, University of Virginia, 1972. The
    most thorough survey of Johnston's suffrage activities and their relation
    to her interest in other reform movements.
HARTLEY, GAYLE MELTON. "The Novels of Mary Johnston: A Critical Study."
    Diss., University of South Carolina 1972. Primarily plot summary and
    extensive quotations; argues Johnston's "most powerful novels" are
    those which reveal her mystical philosophy, but does not identify the
    source of her belief.

HUBBELL, JAY B. "Cavalier and Indentured Servant in Virginia Fiction." *South Atlantic Quarterly* 26 (1927): 22-39. Skeptical about the authenticity of Johnston's early works, but credits her with influencing other novelists.

LEISY, ERNEST E. *The American Historical Novel.* Norman: University of Oklahoma Press, 1950. Discusses several of Johnston's novels with occasional moderate praise.

LIVELY, ROBERT A. *Fiction Fights the Civil War: An Unfinished Chapter in the Literary History of the American People.* Chapel Hill: University of North Carolina Press, 1957. Several brief references to the novels, stressing their faithfulness to documented fact; categorizes Johnston with Scott as writers of the "true *historical novel.*"

LONGEST, GEORGE C. *Three Virginia Writers; Mary Johnston, Thomas Nelson Page, and Amélie Rives Troubetzkoy: A Reference Guide.* Boston: G. K. Hall & Co., 1978. Especially valuable as a convenient, though not exhaustive, list of reviews; lists all valuable secondary sources, with annotations.

NELSON, LAWRENCE G. "Mary Johnston and the Historic Imagination." In *Southern Writers: Appraisals in Our Time,* ed. R. C. Simonini, Jr. Charlottesville: The University Press of Virginia, 1964. The most balanced and thorough survey of Johnston's career; based on careful research and perceptive reading.

OVERTON, GRANT. "Mary Johnston's Adventures." In *Cargoes for Crusoes.* New York: D. Appleton & Company, 1924. Highly appreciative of Johnston and her work; attempts to characterize her mystical experiences without awareness of important biographical facts.

———. *The Women Who Make Our Novels.* Rev. ed. New York: Dodd, Mead and Company, 1928. Quotes extensively from and preserves errors of earlier work, but has reservations about the effect of mysticism upon her career.

PATTERSON, DOROTHYA RENTFRO. "Mary Johnston as a Novelist." M.A. thesis, Southern Methodist University 1941. Reasonable though brief evaluations of the works, incorporating comments of reviewers.

QUINN, ARTHUR HOBSON. *American Fiction: An Historical and Critical Survey.* New York: D. Appleton-Century Co., 1936. Representative of scholarship's consensus view of Johnston's career.

ROBERSON, JOHN R. "Two Virginia Novelists on Woman's Suffrage." *Virginia Magazine of History and Biography* 64: 3 (1956): 286-90. The subtitle, "An exchange of Letters between Mary Johnston and Thomas Nelson Page," epitomizes the work.

RUBIN, LOUIS D., JR. "The Image of an Army: The Civil War in Southern Fiction." In *Virginia in History and Tradition,* ed. R. C. Simonini, Jr. Farmville, Va.: Longwood College, 1958. Offers moderate praise of Johnston's works while arguing that no Southern writer has provided the introspective view necessary for effective treatment of the war.

SHERMAN, CAROLINE B. "The Rediscovery of Mary Johnston (1870-1936)."
    Southern Literary Messenger N.S. 4 (1942): 431-32. Brief survey of the
    works by topics; claims without verification that the works were
    undergoing a revival.
VAN AUKEN, SHELDON. "The Southern Historical Novel in the Early Twen-
    tieth Century." *Journal of Southern History* 14 (1948): 157-91. Argues
    that *Lewis Rand* and the Civil War novels form a trilogy; praises
    Johnston's authenticity and detail.
WAGENKNECHT, EDWARD. "Allotropes and Mary Johnston." In *Cavalcade of
    the American Novel: From the Birth of the Nation to the Middle of
    the Twentieth Century.* New York: Henry Holt and Company, 1952.
    Largely a recapitulation, often in the same phraseology, of the next
    item.
————. "The World and Mary Johnston." *Sewanee Review* 44 (April-June
    1936): 188-206. Unconvincing in its emphasis upon the importance of
    the mystical works, but valuable for critical insights and as a general
    survey of themes and ideas.
WOODBRIDGE, ANNIE. "Mary Johnston on War: An Unpublished Letter and
    a Comment." *Jack London Newsletter* 11 (January - April 1978): 31-
    32. Stresses the distaste for all wars evident in Johnston's reply to a
    letter about *Cease Firing;* the letter, dated June 20, 1913, also confirms
    Johnston's interest in eugenics.

Index